INFOGRAPHIC

|||||||||||||||||||||||||||||||||||||||||||||||||| **GUIDE TO** ||||||||||||||||||||||||||||||||||||||||||||||||||

MUSIC

An Hachette UK Company
www.hachette.co.uk

First published in Great Britain in 2014 by Cassell Illustrated
a division of Octopus Publishing Group Ltd

Endeavour House
189 Shaftesbury Avenue
London
WC2H 8JY

www.octopusbooks.co.uk
www.octopusbooksusa.com

Copyright © Essential Works Ltd 2014

Distributed in the US by
Hachette Book Group USA
237 Park Avenue
New York NY 10017 USA

Distributed in Canada by
Canadian Manda Group
664 Annette Street
Toronto, Ontario, Canada M6S 2C8

ISBN 978-1-844037-53-7

A CIP catalogue record for this book is available from the British Library

Printed and bound in China

1 3 5 7 9 10 8 6 4 2

INFOGRAPHIC
GUIDE TO
MUSIC

Graham Betts

CONTENTS

Introduction

by Graham Betts

According to conventional wisdom, statistics can be used to prove almost
anything. While it is certainly true that facts and figures lend credence to many
an argument, my own experiences are that they are invariably trotted out to
support an otherwise flawed case. Having spent the majority of my working
life in the music business I can safely say that record companies are not averse
to adapting statistics to suit their marketing needs. In the music business,
success is gauged almost entirely on whether Record A sells more in a week
than Record B, and therefore attains a higher chart peak. Of course, timing in
the record industry is almost as important as talent – had certain well-known
singles by major artists been issued three months either side of their official
release, the chances are they would have made number one instead of being the
bridesmaids to far less well-remembered hits by bands who swiftly disappeared
from the scene. In certain cases, as you'll discover inside this book, there are
internationally renowned, major recording artists who never had a Number 1 hit
in America during their long and illustrious careers.

You can perhaps understand why we looked at presenting a completely different
array of facts and figures in this collection of Infographics. Investigating
who has accumulated the biggest pop fortune is fun, but it is made all the
more interesting when you take into account how quickly some of the artists
made their fortunes. And, if you look at one of the other Infographics, you
will appreciate that every £100 million the artist has earned is merely a small
percentage of what the record company has cleared. Although it's certainly
more than the artists could have ever earned if they had stuck to their original
day job, the subject of another of our graphics.

I have to admit that, in some cases, we could have expanded the listings. Take
for example the list of famous rappers who have been the victims of shootings,
sometimes self-inflicted. It is not only rappers, for we could have gone back as

far as Johnny Ace (shot himself playing Russian roulette), Sam Cooke or John Lennon, and included them as well. Our listing, however, concentrates on those who have survived their various brushes with firearms (although ODB subsequently died from a drugs overdose) to boast about it in rhyme. Sadly, though, we simply couldn't fit every bit of information that we have about the music business, music, recordings and instruments into one book – although we have a great graphic on the timeline of the electric guitar, and another comparing the on-stage equipment used by The Beatles at Shea Stadium in 1965 with that of a recent Paul McCartney world tour.

What we have attempted to do is to address some familiar topics about all types of popular music, and to highlight some aspects that are not so usually discussed. For instance, from time to time debate will rage over what is to be considered the very first rock 'n' roll record, with all manner of obscure discs being put forward as older than the last one considered as the rightful instigator of the musical style. We are not about to add fuel to that particular fire but rather start a whole new one – what was the very first disco record? Irrespective of your choice (and there is a significant difference of opinion on this particular genre, too), we've put together a disco timeline that will bring back some memories of past dances, fads and fashions. Of course, one of the main components of the disco movement was the 12" single, and it will also be noted that vinyl is making something of a comeback, and that's the subject of another of our Infographics.

Overall, though, we hope there is an interesting mix of musical history, opinions and the obscure to be gleaned from scrutinizing the graphics inside. You can discover what ZZ Top have on their minds, what percentage of a CD sale finds its way into the record company coffers, which Beatle has been more successful since they split, the top hip-hop stars of the genre, how it feels to be James Brown, Bob Dylan's fluctuating cool quotient and the effect that Bono has had on the Irish population growth of the past four decades. Plus much, much more.

If music is the food of love, then prepare to gorge yourself on a full smorgasbord in this one, easy-to-digest volume.

[SAT]URDAY
[NI]GHT **FEVER**

[Thr]oughout the 1970s disco music grew
[to beco]me the dominant sound on dance
[floors a]nd radios around the world.
[See h]ow the music and
[scene d]eveloped.

The Loft opened in New York
by David Mancuso in February

Move On Up – Curtis Mayfield
Get Up (I Feel Like Being a) Sex Machine –
James Brown

1970 ===== ## 1971 =====

Funky Nassau –
Beginning Of The End
Theme From Shaft –
Isaac Hayes

Don't Go Breaking My Heart –
Elton John & Kiki Dee

First commercial 12" release *Ten
Percent* by Double Exposure

December 14
Saturday Night Fever
film opens

[1]977 =====   ## 1976 =====

*Dance Dance Dance
(Yowsah, Yowsah, Yowsah)* –
Chic

for 8 weeks

#1 *You Should Be Dancing* –
The Bee Gees

Studio 54 opened on
W 54th St in New York

for 1 week

Van McCoy's
The Hustle
becomes the
biggest
dance craze
in disco

Village People formed, bring in
HiNRG (electronic disco music)

[1]978

[Le Fre]*ak* – Chic

7 million worldwide

Heart Of Glass – Blondie
Copacabana – Barry Manilow
Miss You – The Rolling Stones

Rock The Boat – Hues Corporation
Keep On Truckin' – Eddie Kendricks

1972

Soul Makossa – Manu Dibango
One Night Affair – Jerry Butler

1973

First **12" single** release:
The promo copy of Swamp Dogg's
Straight From My Heart

Rolling Stone publishes first
article about disco by Vince
Aletti in September

#1

Bad Luck – Harold Melvin
& The Blue Notes

for 11 weeks

1975

Remixer Tom Moulton cuts 12"
single of *I'll Be Holding On*
by Al Dowling

Fatback Band release
(Are You Ready) Do The Bus Stop

1974

Rock Your Baby – George McCrae
Kung Fu Fighting – Carl Douglas

11 million worldwide

Billboard launches first chart, Disco Action,
on October 26 (*Never Can Say Goodbye* by
Gloria Gaynor first chart topper).

First disco radio show – WPIX-FM runs
Disco 102 from November (NY, USA)

Gloria Gaynor's *I Will
Survive* is the lead
release, for which she
wins a Grammy.
July 12 *Disco Demolition
Night* is held – in Chicago
people bring disco records
along to be burned on the
baseball field

June 20 – *Can't Stop
The Music* film opens.
February 4 –
Studio 54 closed

Million selling

ALBUM of the YEAR

5 million approx

1979

I Will Survive – Gloria Gaynor
Hot Stuff & *Bad Girls* – Donna Summer

1980

*A Lover's Holiday/
The Glow Of Love/
Searching* – Change

Another One Bites The Dust – Queen

Disco, The Music, The Times, The Era, Johnny Morgan, Sterling 2011

TAKE IT TO THE **BANK**

The richest artists in the music business don't make
their money just by writing, singing and performing.
They also invest in other businesses, as shown here.

Artist	Value
Andrew Lloyd Webber	$1.2B
Paul McCartney (The Beatles/Wings)	$800M
Herb Alpert (Tijuana Brass) — (A&M)	$730M
Madonna — (Maverick)	$650M
Bono (Paul Hewson) (U2)	$600M
Bing Crosby	$550M
Puff Daddy (Sean Combs) — (Bad Boy Records)	$550M
Mariah Carey	$500M
Emilio Estefan (Miami Sound Machine)	$500M
Jay-Z (Jason Carter)	$470M
Dolly Parton — (Dollywood)	$450M
Jimmy Buffet	$400M
Michael Jackson	$350M
Garth Brooks	$325M
Gene Autry	$320M
Mick Jagger (The Rolling Stones)	$305M
Gene Simmons (Kiss)	$300M

OTHER INTERESTS

- Theatre production
- Music publishing
- Record label
- Property
- Radio
- Television
- Horses
- Acting
- Music production
- Endorsements
- Restaurants
- Writing
- Theme parks
- Brewing
- Fundraising
- Radio stations
- Baseball
- Film production
- Car dealership
- Inherited wealth
- Branded headphones
- Filmmaking
- Charity
- Music management
- Yacht rental
- Songwriting collaborations

Name	Interest label	Net worth
Beyoncé		$300M
Elton John		$300M
Ringo Starr (The Beatles)		$300M
Antonio 'L.A.' Reid (The Deele)	(LaFace)	$300M
Elvis Presley		$300M
Sting (Gordon Sumner) (The Police)		$240M
Keith Richards (The Rolling Stones)		$280M
Dhani Harrison (son of George Harrison)		$275M
Dr Dre (Andre Young) (N.W.A.)	(Death Row)	$250M
50 Cent (Curtis Jackson)		$250M
Prince (Prince Nelson)		$250M
Tim Rice		$230M
Dave Grohl (Nirvana/Foo Fighters)		$225M
Sean Lennon (son of John Lennon)		$200M
Bruce Springsteen		$200M
Don Henley (The Eagles)		$200M
Eric Clapton (Yardbirds/Cream)		$200M

wikipedia.org, forbes.com, celebritynetworth.com

13

RECORD COMPANY
HISTORICAL MAP

Almost since it began the music industry has been fiercely competitive, and over the course of 125 years there have been numerous takeovers, new company successes and battles over market dominance. Today there are only 3 record labels left in the world.

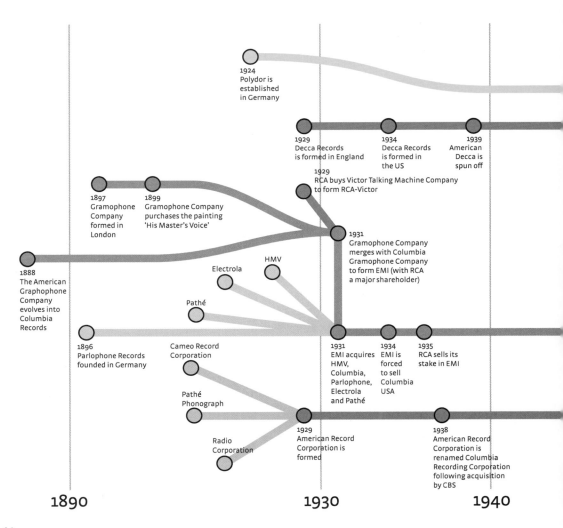

1924
Polydor is established in Germany

1929
Decca Records is formed in England

1934
Decca Records is formed in the US

1939
American Decca is spun off

1929
RCA buys Victor Talking Machine Company to form RCA-Victor

1897
Gramophone Company formed in London

1899
Gramophone Company purchases the painting 'His Master's Voice'

HMV

Electrola

1931
Gramophone Company merges with Columbia Gramophone Company to form EMI (with RCA a major shareholder)

Pathé

1888
The American Graphophone Company evolves into Columbia Records

1896
Parlophone Records founded in Germany

Cameo Record Corporation

1931
EMI acquires HMV, Columbia, Parlophone, Electrola and Pathé

1934
EMI is forced to sell Columbia USA

1935
RCA sells its stake in EMI

Pathé Phonograph

Radio Corporation

1929
American Record Corporation is formed

1938
American Record Corporation is renamed Columbia Recording Corporation following acquisition by CBS

1890

1930

1940

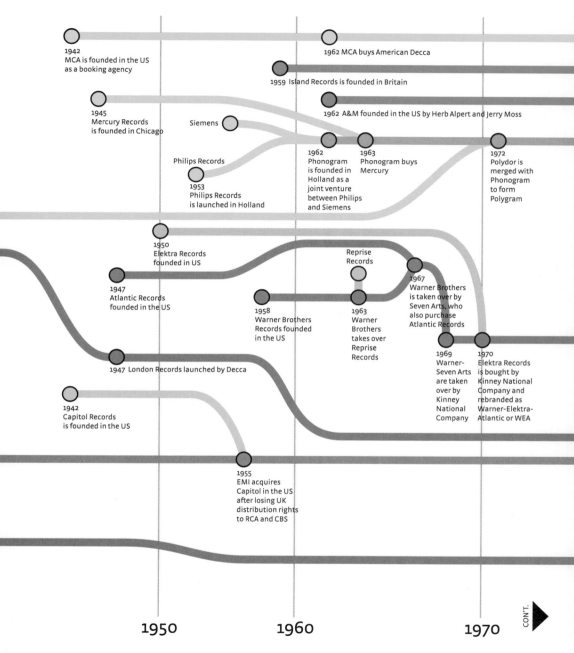

1942 MCA is founded in the US as a booking agency

1962 MCA buys American Decca

1959 Island Records is founded in Britain

1945 Mercury Records is founded in Chicago

Siemens

1962 A&M founded in the US by Herb Alpert and Jerry Moss

Philips Records

1962 Phonogram is founded in Holland as a joint venture between Philips and Siemens

1963 Phonogram buys Mercury

1972 Polydor is merged with Phonogram to form Polygram

1953 Philips Records is launched in Holland

1950 Elektra Records founded in US

Reprise Records

1947 Atlantic Records founded in the US

1967 Warner Brothers is taken over by Seven Arts, who also purchase Atlantic Records

1958 Warner Brothers Records founded in the US

1963 Warner Brothers takes over Reprise Records

1969 Warner-Seven Arts are taken over by Kinney National Company

1970 Elektra Records is bought by Kinney National Company and rebranded as Warner-Elektra-Atlantic or WEA

1947 London Records launched by Decca

1942 Capitol Records is founded in the US

1955 EMI acquires Capitol in the US after losing UK distribution rights to RCA and CBS

1950   **1960**   **1970**

CON'T.

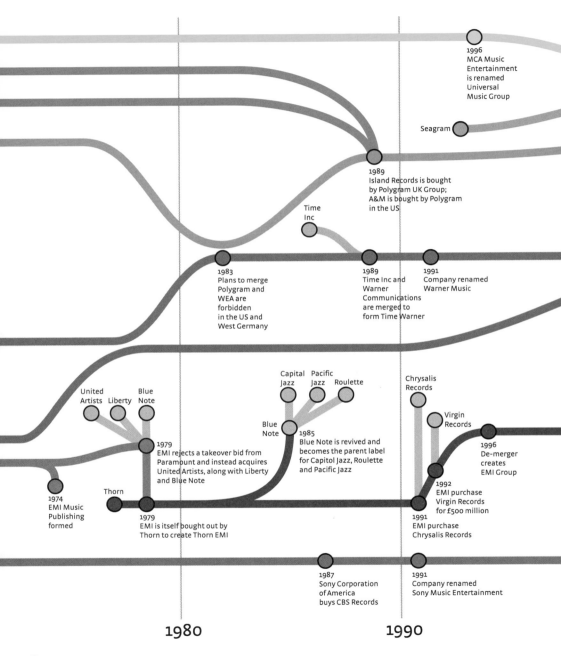

1996
MCA Music
Entertainment
is renamed
Universal
Music Group

Seagram

1989
Island Records is bought
by Polygram UK Group;
A&M is bought by Polygram
in the US

Time
Inc

1983
Plans to merge
Polygram and
WEA are
forbidden
in the US and
West Germany

1989
Time Inc and
Warner
Communications
are merged to
form Time Warner

1991
Company renamed
Warner Music

Capital Pacific
Jazz Jazz Roulette

Chrysalis
Records

United
Artists Liberty Blue
Note

Blue
Note

Virgin
Records

1985
Blue Note is revived and
becomes the parent label
for Capitol Jazz, Roulette
and Pacific Jazz

1996
De-merger
creates
EMI Group

1979
EMI rejects a takeover bid from
Paramount and instead acquires
United Artists, along with Liberty
and Blue Note

1992
EMI purchase
Virgin Records
for £500 million

1974
EMI Music
Publishing
formed

Thorn

1979
EMI is itself bought out by
Thorn to create Thorn EMI

1991
EMI purchase
Chrysalis Records

1987
Sony Corporation
of America
buys CBS Records

1991
Company renamed
Sony Music Entertainment

1980

1990

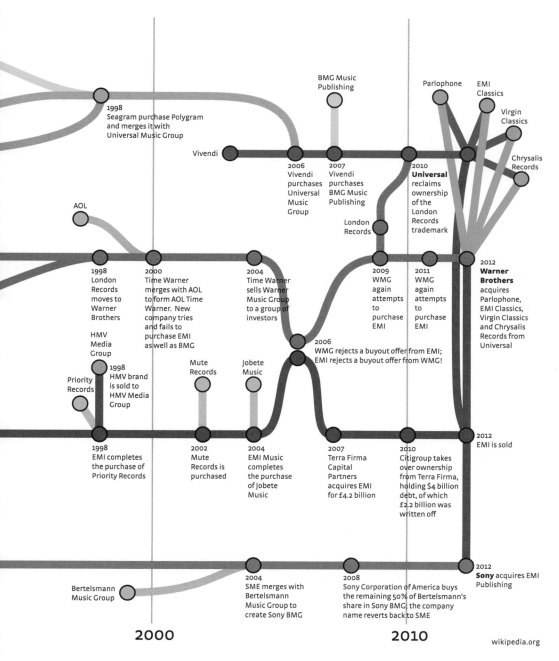

BMG Music
Publishing

Parlophone

EMI
Classics

Virgin
Classics

1998
Seagram purchase Polygram
and merges it with
Universal Music Group

Vivendi

2006
Vivendi
purchases
Universal
Music
Group

2007
Vivendi
purchases
BMG Music
Publishing

2010
Universal
reclaims
ownership
of the
London
Records
trademark

Chrysalis
Records

AOL

London
Records

1998
London
Records
moves to
Warner
Brothers

2000
Time Warner
merges with AOL
to form AOL Time
Warner. New
company tries
and fails to
purchase EMI
as well as BMG

2004
Time Warner
sells Warner
Music Group
to a group of
investors

2009
WMG
again
attempts
to
purchase
EMI

2011
WMG
again
attempts
to
purchase
EMI

2012
**Warner
Brothers**
acquires
Parlophone,
EMI Classics,
Virgin Classics
and Chrysalis
Records from
Universal

HMV
Media
Group

Priority
Records

1998
HMV brand
is sold to
HMV Media
Group

Mute
Records

Jobete
Music

2006
WMG rejects a buyout offer from EMI;
EMI rejects a buyout offer from WMG!

2012
EMI is sold

1998
EMI completes
the purchase of
Priority Records

2002
Mute
Records is
purchased

2004
EMI Music
completes
the purchase
of Jobete
Music

2007
Terra Firma
Capital
Partners
acquires EMI
for £4.2 billion

2010
Citigroup takes
over ownership
from Terra Firma,
holding $4 billion
debt, of which
£2.2 billion was
written off

Bertelsmann
Music Group

2004
SME merges with
Bertelsmann
Music Group to
create Sony BMG

2008
Sony Corporation of America buys
the remaining 50% of Bertelsmann's
share in Sony BMG; the company
name reverts back to SME

2012
Sony acquires EMI
Publishing

2000

2010

wikipedia.org

17

ELVIS **DONUT**

For 24 years Elvis Presley recorded, acted and performed on stage, on screen and in the studio. Here's how his two dozen years as a professional performer add up.

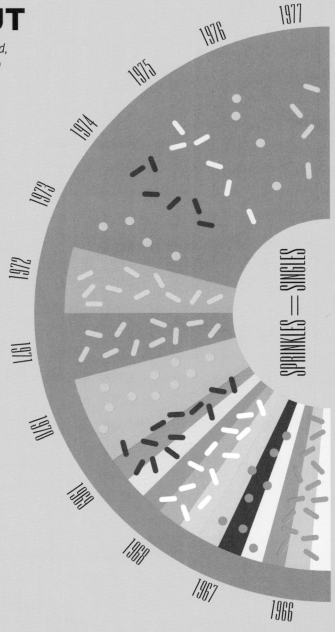

SPRINKLES = SINGLES

1977 · 1976 · 1975 · 1974 · 1973 · 1972 · 1971 · 1970 · 1969 · 1968 · 1967 · 1966

LIVE DATES

52 1954	**327** 1955	**236** 1956
28 1957	**3** 1961	**57** 1969
145 1970	**128** 1971	**165** 1972
146 1973	**127** 1974	**101** 1975
112 1976	**59** 1977	

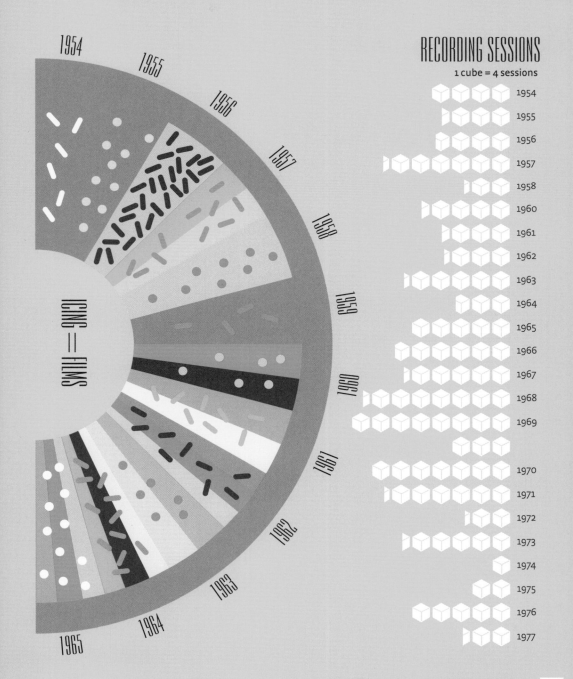

Essential Elvis, Peter Silverton, 2013, Rocket 88 Books, wikipedia.org

ACHTUNG **BABIES**

*The Irish solution to the population explosion: every year that U2 released a new album,
Ireland's birth rate dropped. And when The Corrs released a new album, it went up.*

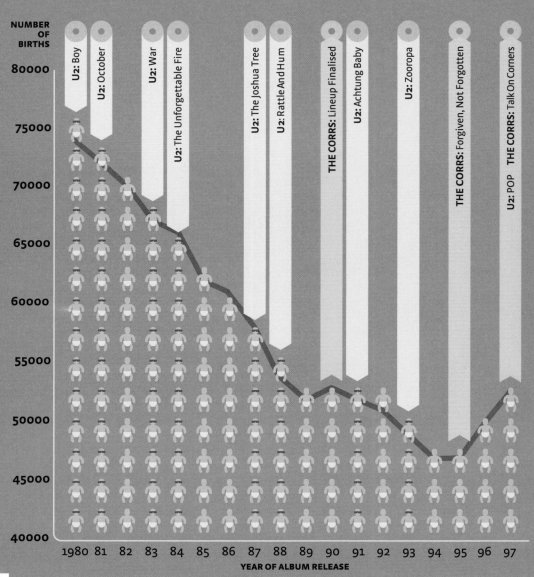

NUMBER
OF
BIRTHS

- U2: Boy
- U2: October
- U2: War
- U2: The Unforgettable Fire
- U2: The Joshua Tree
- U2: Rattle And Hum
- THE CORRS: Lineup Finalised
- U2: Achtung Baby
- U2: Zooropa
- THE CORRS: Forgiven, Not Forgotten
- U2: POP
- THE CORRS: Talk On Corners

80000
75000
70000
65000
60000
55000
50000
45000
40000

1980 81 82 83 84 85 86 87 88 89 90 91 92 93 94 95 96 97

YEAR OF ALBUM RELEASE

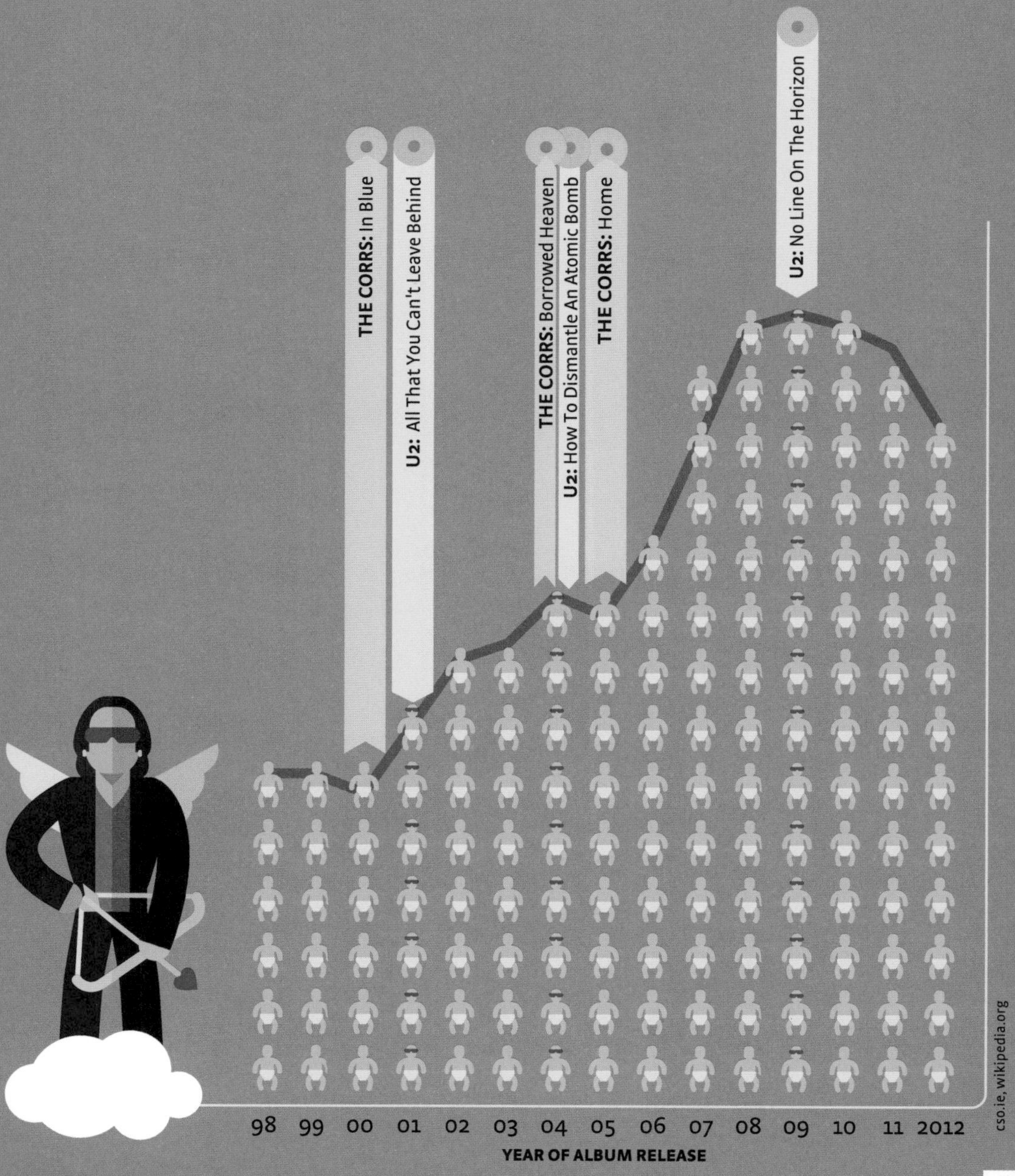

THE CORRS: In Blue

U2: All That You Can't Leave Behind

THE CORRS: Borrowed Heaven

U2: How To Dismantle An Atomic Bomb

THE CORRS: Home

U2: No Line On The Horizon

98 99 00 01 02 03 04 05 06 07 08 09 10 11 2012

YEAR OF ALBUM RELEASE

cso.ie, wikipedia.org

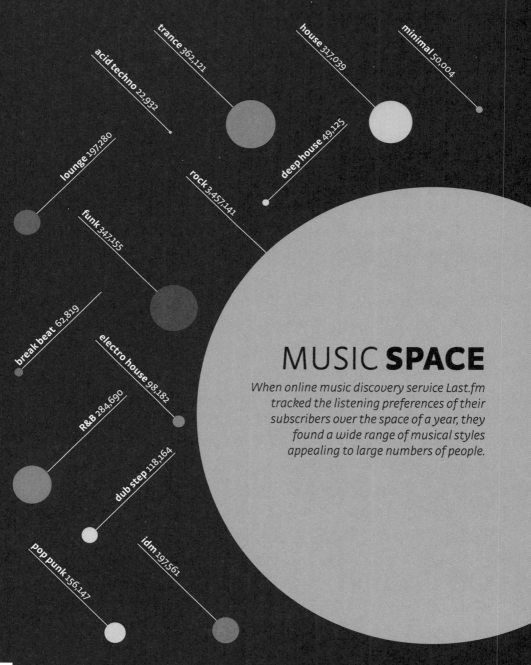

trance 362,121

acid techno 22,932

house 317,039

minimal 50,004

lounge 197,280

deep house 49,125

rock 3,457,141

funk 347,155

break beat 62,819

electro house 98,182

R&B 284,690

dub step 118,164

pop punk 156,147

idm 197,561

MUSIC **SPACE**

When online music discovery service Last.fm tracked the listening preferences of their subscribers over the space of a year, they found a wide range of musical styles appealing to large numbers of people.

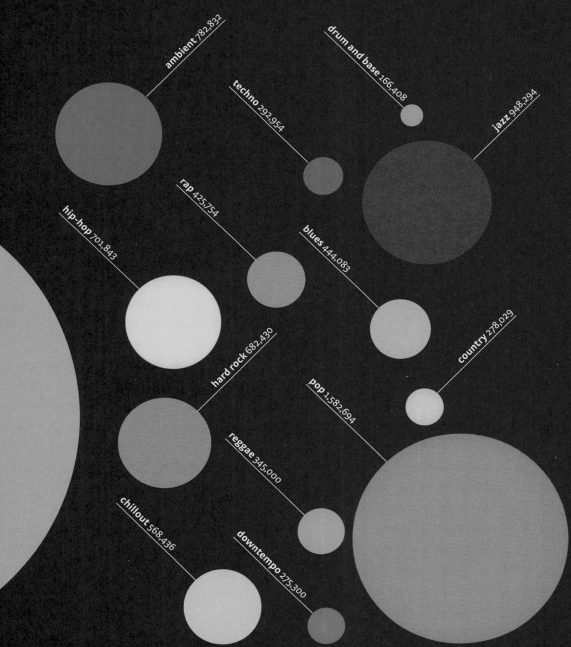

ambient 782.832

drum and base 166,408

techno 292,954

jazz 948,294

rap 425,754

hip-hop 701,843

blues 444,083

country 278,029

hard rock 682,430

pop 1,582,694

reggae 345,000

chillout 568,436

downtempo 275,300

LastFM.com

23

THE HEIGHT OF POP **SUCCESS**

Measuring the height of musicians and their record sales, the smaller you are as a solo singer, the more likely you are to be a bigger hit, but to be a successful band member you should be taller to gain more success. That is, unless you are AC/DC, who are by far and away the smallest group of musical individuals to achieve massive sales success.

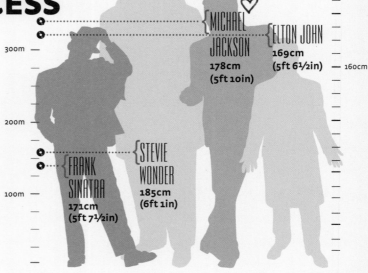

Male soloists

MICHAEL JACKSON
178cm
(5ft 10in)

ELTON JOHN
169cm
(5ft 6½in)

FRANK SINATRA
171cm
(5ft 7½in)

STEVIE WONDER
185cm
(6ft 1in)

— 180cm
— 160cm

300m —
200m —
100m —

Bands

*Shortest and most successful band member is **Angus Young** of **AC/DC** at 157cm (5ft 2in); tallest is **Brian May** (**Queen**) who is 185cm (6ft 1in).*

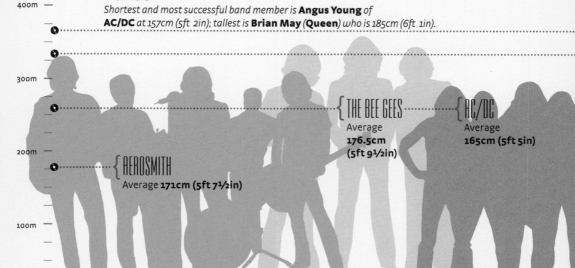

400m —
300m —
200m —
100m —

THE BEE GEES
Average
176.5cm
(5ft 9½in)

AC/DC
Average
165cm (5ft 5in)

AEROSMITH
Average **171cm** (5ft 7½in)

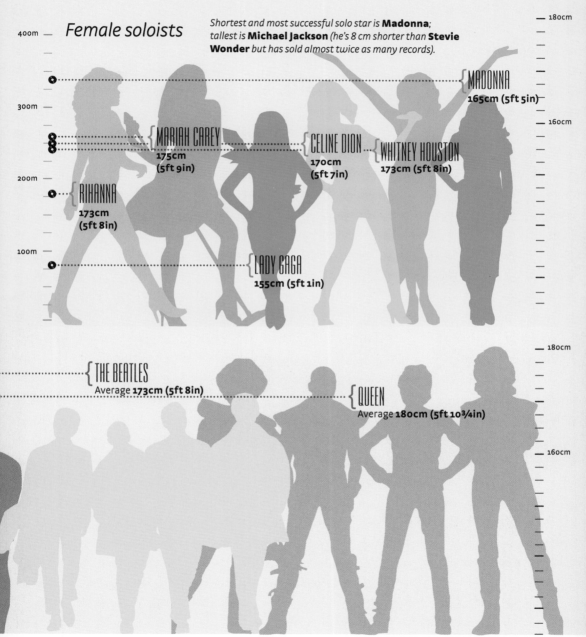

Female soloists

Shortest and most successful solo star is **Madonna**; *tallest is* **Michael Jackson** *(he's 8 cm shorter than* **Stevie Wonder** *but has sold almost twice as many records).*

400m

300m

200m

100m

180cm

160cm

MADONNA
165cm (5ft 5in)

MARIAH CAREY
175cm
(5ft 9in)

CELINE DION
170cm
(5ft 7in)

WHITNEY HOUSTON
173cm (5ft 8in)

RIHANNA
173cm
(5ft 8in)

LADY GAGA
155cm (5ft 1in)

180cm

160cm

THE BEATLES
Average **173cm (5ft 8in)**

QUEEN
Average **180cm (5ft 10¾in)**

WHAT'S ON
ZZ TOP'S MIND?

*The Texan trio have recorded and released 162 songs
across 15 studio albums between 1971 and 2012.
Breaking down the subject matter of the songs
reveals their main trains of thought to be about:*

SUBJECT	NUMBER OF SONGS	% TOTAL
women and/or sex	74	46
travel and/or cars	27	17
the blues	9	5.6
alcohol and/or food	9	5.6
money	6	3.6
lost love	6	3.6
gambling	4	2.5
partying/clubbing	3	1.9
a life of crime	2	1.2
other (monsters, ageing, partying, neighbours, the weather, drugs, the Devil, homosexuality in jail, sin, teddy bears, clothes, concrete and steel, pincushions, surfing, lizards, Vincent Price, dread, religion, stupidity, Chartreuse, settling down)	21	13

discogs.com

27

MAKING TRACKS TO THE
PROMISED LAND

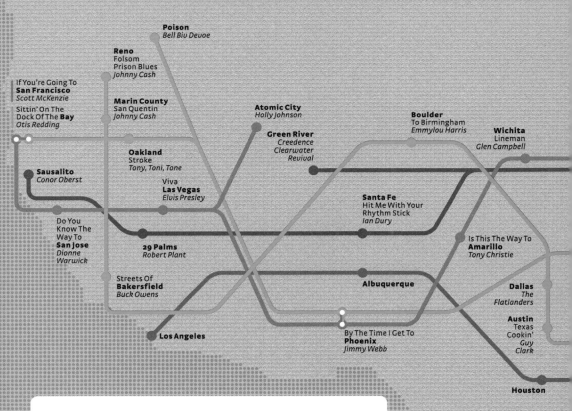

Poison
Bell Biv Devoe

Reno
Folsom
Prison Blues
Johnny Cash

If You're Going To
San Francisco
Scott McKenzie

Sittin' On The
Dock Of The **Bay**
Otis Redding

Marin County
San Quentin
Johnny Cash

Atomic City
Holly Johnson

Boulder
To Birmingham
Emmylou Harris

Green River
*Creedence
Clearwater
Revival*

Wichita
Lineman
Glen Campbell

Sausalito
Conor Oberst

Oakland
Stroke
Tony, Toni, Tone

Viva
Las Vegas
Elvis Presley

Santa Fe
Hit Me With Your
Rhythm Stick
Ian Dury

Do You
Know The
Way To
San Jose
*Dionne
Warwick*

29 Palms
Robert Plant

Is This The Way To
Amarillo
Tony Christie

Streets Of
Bakersfield
Buck Owens

Albuquerque

Dallas
*The
Flatlanders*

Austin
Texas
Cookin'
*Guy
Clark*

Los Angeles

By The Time I Get To
Phoenix
Jimmy Webb

Houston

Chuck Berry's The Promised Land (1964) cruises through
real places in America from the East Coast to the West.
Other places – cities, towns, inlets, rivers, bridges
and docks – across the country have been
similarly immortalized in songs. Here's a route
map for one great musical tour of the States.

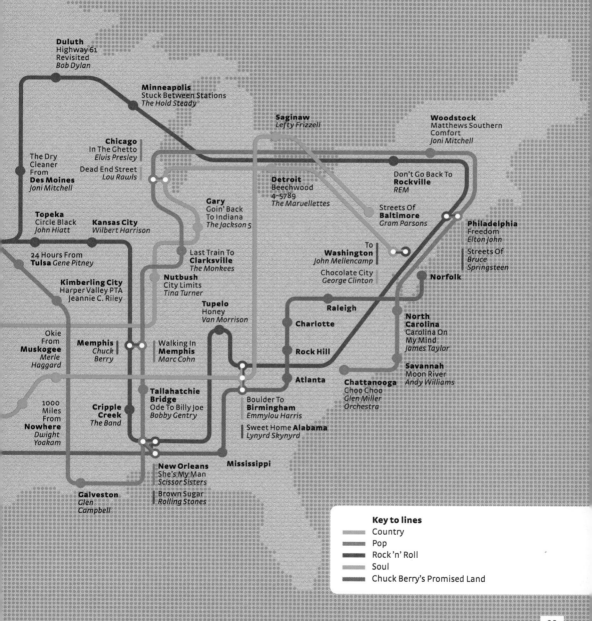

Duluth
Highway 61 Revisited
Bob Dylan

Minneapolis
Stuck Between Stations
The Hold Steady

Saginaw
Lefty Frizzell

Woodstock
Matthews Southern Comfort
Joni Mitchell

Chicago
In The Ghetto
Elvis Presley
Dead End Street
Lou Rawls

The Dry Cleaner From
Des Moines
Joni Mitchell

Don't Go Back To
Rockville
REM

Detroit
Beechwood 4-5789
The Marvellettes

Gary
Goin' Back To Indiana
The Jackson 5

Streets Of
Baltimore
Gram Parsons

Philadelphia
Freedom
Elton John

Topeka
Circle Black
John Hiatt

Kansas City
Wilbert Harrison

24 Hours From
Tulsa *Gene Pitney*

Last Train To
Clarksville
The Monkees

To
Washington
John Mellencamp

Chocolate City
George Clinton

Streets Of
Bruce Springsteen

Norfolk

Kimberling City
Harper Valley PTA
Jeannie C. Riley

Nutbush
City Limits
Tina Turner

Tupelo
Honey
Van Morrison

Raleigh

Charlotte

North Carolina
Carolina On My Mind
James Taylor

Okie From
Muskogee
Merle Haggard

Memphis
Chuck Berry

Walking In
Memphis
Marc Cohn

Rock Hill

Savannah
Moon River
Andy Williams

1000 Miles From
Nowhere
Dwight Yoakam

Cripple Creek
The Band

Tallahatchie Bridge
Ode To Billy Joe
Bobby Gentry

Atlanta

Boulder To
Birmingham
Emmylou Harris

Chattanooga
Choo Choo
Glen Miller Orchestra

Sweet Home **Alabama**
Lynyrd Skynyrd

New Orleans
She's My Man
Scissor Sisters

Mississippi

Galveston
Glen Campbell

Brown Sugar
Rolling Stones

Key to lines
— Country
— Pop
— Rock 'n' Roll
— Soul
— Chuck Berry's Promised Land

THE **NOT ONLY** 27 CLUB

The 27 Club is made up with musicians who died at the age of 27. The unlucky 13 make up just a small part of musician heaven, though.

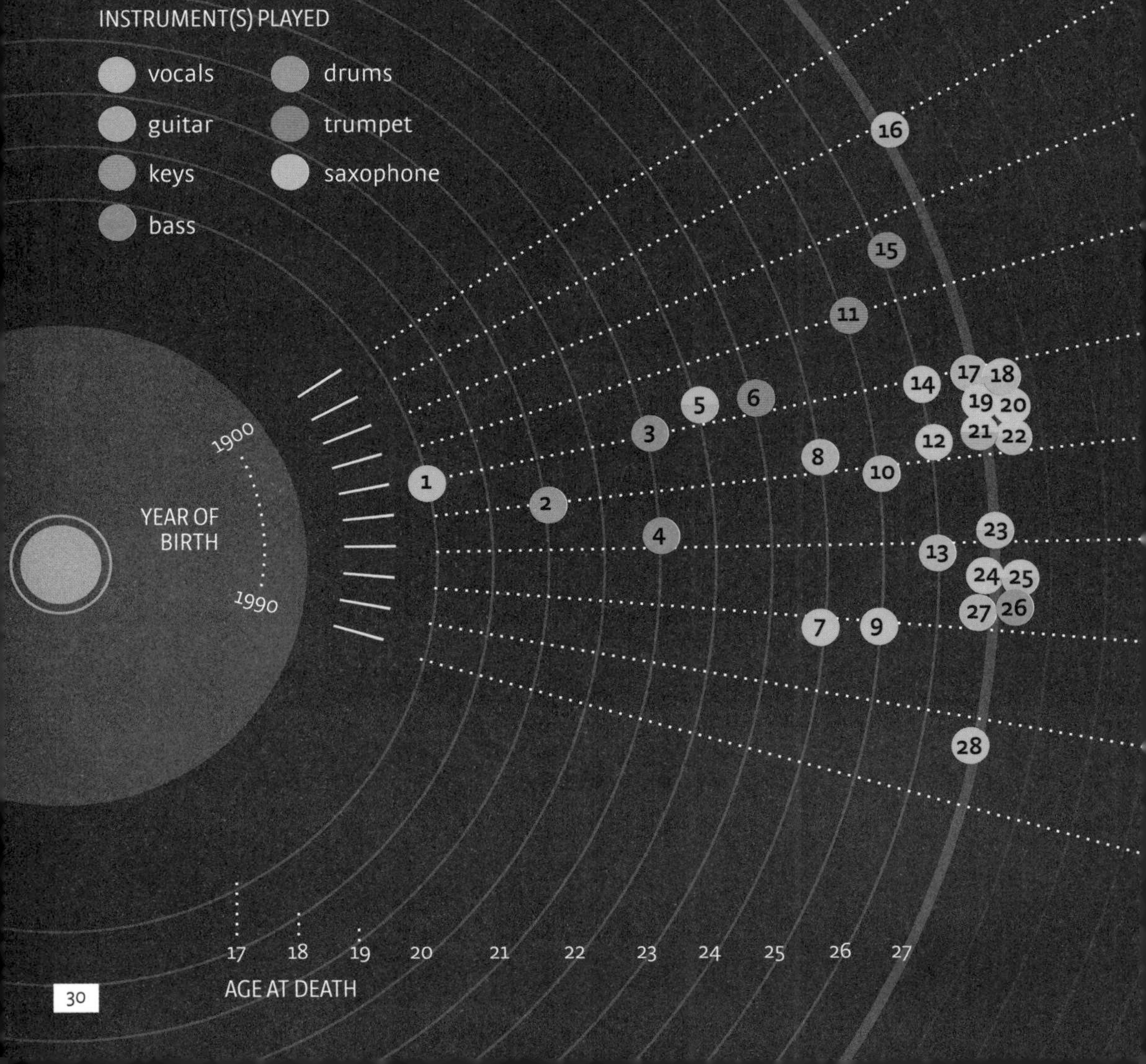

INSTRUMENT(S) PLAYED

- vocals
- guitar
- keys
- bass
- drums
- trumpet
- saxophone

YEAR OF BIRTH

1900

1990

16

15

11

14 17 18
19 20
12 21 22

5 6

3
8 10

1
23
2
13 24 25
4
27 26
7 9

28

17   18   19   20   21   22   23   24   25   26   27

AGE AT DEATH

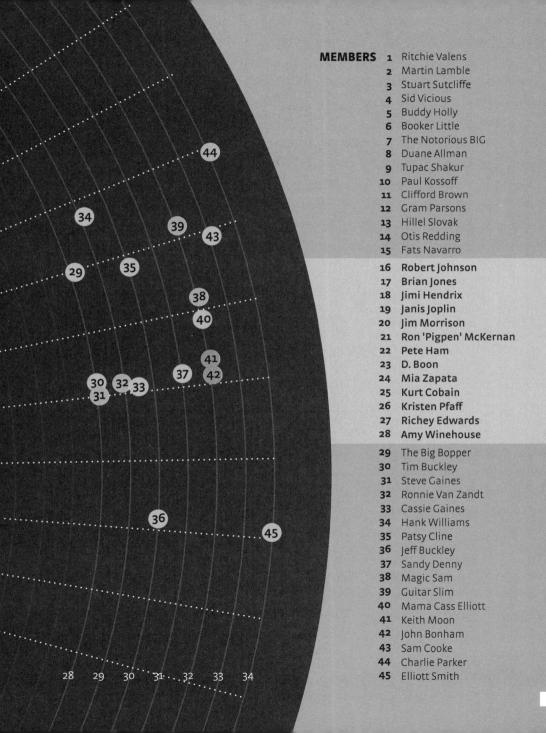

MEMBERS

1 Ritchie Valens
2 Martin Lamble
3 Stuart Sutcliffe
4 Sid Vicious
5 Buddy Holly
6 Booker Little
7 The Notorious BIG
8 Duane Allman
9 Tupac Shakur
10 Paul Kossoff
11 Clifford Brown
12 Gram Parsons
13 Hillel Slovak
14 Otis Redding
15 Fats Navarro

16 **Robert Johnson**
17 **Brian Jones**
18 **Jimi Hendrix**
19 **Janis Joplin**
20 **Jim Morrison**
21 **Ron 'Pigpen' McKernan**
22 **Pete Ham**
23 **D. Boon**
24 **Mia Zapata**
25 **Kurt Cobain**
26 **Kristen Pfaff**
27 **Richey Edwards**
28 **Amy Winehouse**

29 The Big Bopper
30 Tim Buckley
31 Steve Gaines
32 Ronnie Van Zandt
33 Cassie Gaines
34 Hank Williams
35 Patsy Cline
36 Jeff Buckley
37 Sandy Denny
38 Magic Sam
39 Guitar Slim
40 Mama Cass Elliott
41 Keith Moon
42 John Bonham
43 Sam Cooke
44 Charlie Parker
45 Elliott Smith

WHO **WRITES** THE SONGS?

These are the most successful songwriters of the past six decades, their best-known titles, and the total number of units sold of all their work.

Best Known For – **Biggest Hit** **sales estimate** Team	*Elvis Presley* – **Jailhouse Rock** **80 million** Jerry Leiber/Mike Stoller
Elvis Presley – **A Teenager In Love** **100 million** Doc Pomus/Mort Shuman	*The Everly Brothers* **Wake Up Little Susie** **200 million** Felice Bryant/Boudleaux Bryant
The Beatles – **Yesterday** **1.5 billion** John Lennon/Paul McCartney	*The Supremes* – **Baby Love** **150 million** Brian Holland/Lamont Dozier/Eddie Holland
The Rolling Stones **(I Can't Get No) Satisfaction** **200 million** Mick Jagger/Keith Richards	*Neil Sedaka* **Breaking Up Is Hard to Do** **100 million** Neil Sedaka/Howard Greenfield
The Shirelles **Will You Love Me Tomorrow** **100 million** Gerry Goffin/Carole King	*Righteous Brothers* **You've Lost That Lovin' Feelin'** **150 million** Cynthia Weil/Barry Mann
The Shangri-Las – **Leader Of The Pack** **150 million** Jeff Barry/Ellie Greenwich	*Marvin Gaye* **I Heard It Through The Grapevine** **75 million** Norman Whitfield/Barrett Strong
Elton John – **Candle In The Wind** **300 million** Elton John/Bernie Taupin	*The O'Jays* – **Love Train** **150 million** Kenny Gamble/Leon Huff

1950s   **1960s**   **1970s**

The Stylistics – You Are Everything	Pink Floyd – Another Brick In The Wall
100 million	**250 million**
Thom Bell/Linda Creed	Roger Waters

ABBA – Waterloo	The Bee Gees – Night Fever
150 million	**250 million**
Benny Andersson/Bjorn Ulvaeus	Barry Gibb/Maurice Gibb/Robin Gibb

Bryan Adams — Everything I Do (I Do It For You)	The Eurythmics – Sweet Dreams
100 million	**75 million**
Bryan Adams/Jim Vallance	Dave Stewart/Annie Lennox

Toni Braxton – Unbreak My Heart	Boyz II Men – The End Of The Road
200 million	**75 million**
Diane Warren	Kenneth Edmonds/L.A. Reid

Backstreet Boys – Quit Playing Games	Katy Perry – Firework
100 million	**100 million**
Max Martin/Dennis Pop/Herbie Crichlow	Mikkel S. Eriksen/Tor Erik Hermansen

Katy Perry – I Kissed A Girl	Snoop Dogg – Drop It Like It's Hot
100 million	**75 million**
Lukasz Gottwald/Max Martin	Chad Hugo/Pharrell Williams

Britney Spears – Oops I Did It Again	Rihanna – Umbrella
75 million	**100 million**
Max Martin/Rami Yacoub	Christopher Stewart/Terius Nas

1980s   1990s   2000s

GET DOWN WITH **JAMES BROWN**

The original hardest-working man in show business, Mr Entertainment himself, James Brown, the Godfather of Soul put a lot of himself and his feelings in to his music. Here's how much:

Like getting up 18%

Black & proud 12%

Like getting down 12%

Good 10%

Too funky 9%

Like getting up offa that thing 6%

Like a sex machine 5%

Like doing it to death 5%

Like getting some 4%

Like a man 4%

Real 3%

Like hell down here 3%

Outta sight 2.5%

Like super bad 2%

In a cold sweat 2%

Like bringing it on 1%

Like a baby 1%

Like talkin' loud and
sayin' nothing 0.5%

LP TITLE – RELEASE DATE

OF DISCS | # OF TRACKS | SHORTEST | LONGEST | RUNNING TIME | COVER VERSIONS

 The Clash – 1977
1 | 14 | 1:34 | 6:01 | 35:18 | 1

 Give 'Em Enough Rope – 1978
1 | 10 | 2:35 | 5:14 | 36:57 | 1

 London Calling – 1979
2 | 19 | 1:46 | 5:37 | 65:07 | 3

 Sandinista! – 1980
3 | 36 | 1:41 | 5:45 | 144.09 | 4

 Black Market Clash – 1980
1 | 9 | 2:06 | 7.00 | 34:37 | 4

 Combat Rock – 1982
1 | 12 | 2:32 | 5:30 | 46:21 | 0

POST-FOUNDER MEMBER MICK JONES

 Cut The Crap – 1985
1 | 12 | 2:39 | 3:49 | 38:21 | 0

DISBANDED 1986 (NEVER REFORMED)

LIVE ALBUMS

 From Here To Eternity: Live – 1999
1 | 17 | 1:43 | 7:24 | 57:68 | 2

 Live At Shea Stadium – 2008
1 | 16 | 1:10 | 4:06 | 49:05 | 4

1977-1986 THE CLASH

DRUMS | VOCALS / GUITAR | GUITAR | BASS | KEYBOARD 1979-1982

6 studio albums in 5 years + one after a founder member left, + 2 live albums long after the band ceased to exist.

There have been 7 compilation albums 1988–2013, and 4 boxed sets 1991–2013.

PUNK'S NOT DEAD –
NOR IS PROG ...

When punk arrived on the UK music scene in 1976 the movement's main protagonists, such as The Clash, claimed to be making music as the antithesis to the kind of overblown, pompous progressive rock made by bands like Yes. Long after the dust has settled, here's the recorded legacy of both bands compared.

YES 1969-1981

DRUMS | VOCALS | GUITAR | BASS | KEYBOARD

9 studio albums in 9 years + one after a founder member left, + 2 live albums while the band were existing.

There have been 9 compilation albums 1975–2007, and 8 boxed sets 1991–2013.

Yes – 1969
1 | 8 | 2:53 | 6:54 | 41:17 | 2

Time And A Word – 1970
1 | 8 | 2:06 | 6:34 | 40:06 | 2

The Yes Album – 1971
1 | 6 | 3:17 | 9:41 | 41:44 | 0

Fragile – 1971
1 | 9 | 0:35 | 11:27 | 41:11 | 1

Close To The Edge – 1972
3 | 8:55 | 18:43 | 37:51 | 0

Tales From Topographic Oceans – 1973
2 | 4 | 18:35 | 21:37 | 81:15 | 0

Relayer – 1974
1 | 3 | 9:06 | 21:50 | 40:30 | 0

Going For The One – 1977
1 | 5 | 3:49 | 15:31 | 38:49 | 0

Tomato – 1978
1 | 8 | 2:25 | 7:47 | 41:35 | 0

POST-FOUNDER MEMBER JON ANDERSON

Drama – 1980
1 | 6 | 1:21 | 10:27 | 36:55 | 0

DISBANDED 1981 (REFORMED 1983)

LIVE ALBUMS

Yessongs – 1973
3 | 13 | 2:53 | 18:13 | 129:55 | 1

Yesshows – 1980
2 | 10 | 3:54 | 22:40 | 78:54 | 1

WHY IS IT SO HARD TO GET **A BIG GIG TICKET**?

This ticket allocation for a gig by a major artist at a 14,000 capacity venue in 2013 reveals why fans who don't have the 'right' credit card, can't afford Platinum Tickets and are not fan club members found it impossible to get seats.

Fan club: 21% 3000 tickets

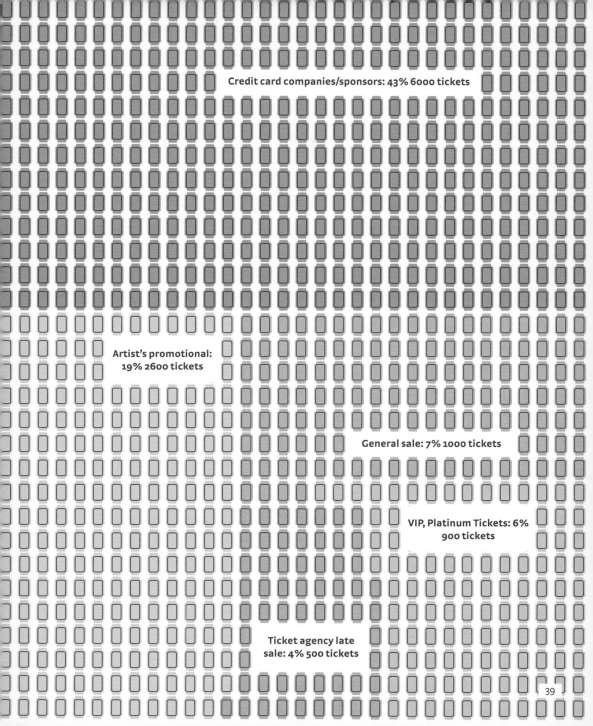

Credit card companies/sponsors: 43% 6000 tickets

Artist's promotional:
19% 2600 tickets

General sale: 7% 1000 tickets

VIP, Platinum Tickets: 6%
900 tickets

Ticket agency late
sale: 4% 500 tickets

39

MJ'S
LIFELINE

Michael Jackson signed his first recording contract at the age of ten and released his first solo album aged 13. By the time of his death aged 50 he'd released ten solo albums and sold over 200 million records. Here's a timeline of those sales.

1971

1972

GOT TO BE THERE

BEN

3,200,000

5,000,000

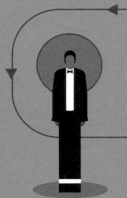

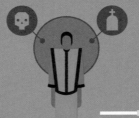

1979

1982

1987

OFF THE WALL

THRILLER

BAD

20,000,000

65,000,000

45,000,000

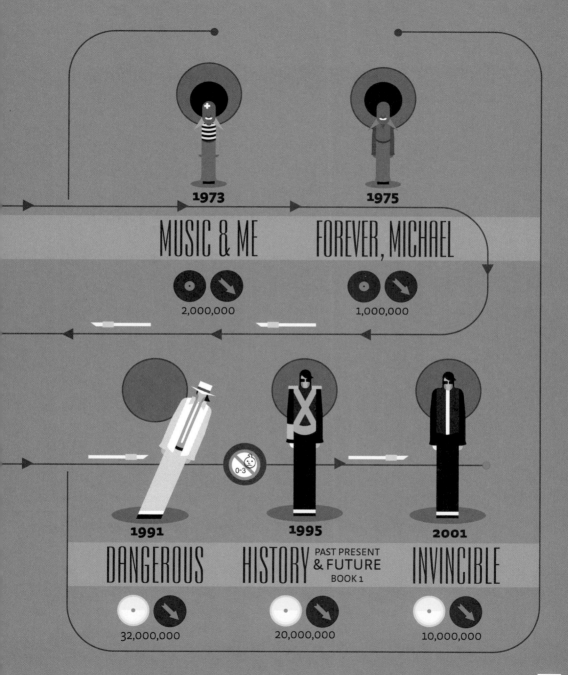

1973

1975

MUSIC & ME

FOREVER, MICHAEL

2,000,000

1,000,000

1991

1995

2001

DANGEROUS

HISTORY PAST PRESENT & FUTURE BOOK 1

INVINCIBLE

32,000,000

20,000,000

10,000,000

THE GOLDEN **KEY**

The great classical composers of the world have generally changed the sound, form and pitch of what was considered the norm for when they were working. It seems that many eminent composers chose a particular key in which they wrote major works. Follow the colours as they represent the percentage use of that key in the composer's music.

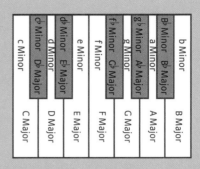

	c♯ Minor	d♯ Minor		f♯ Minor	g♯ Minor	b Minor	
		D♭ Major	E♭ Major			a♯ Minor	b Minor
c Minor	d Minor		e Minor	f Minor	C♯ Major	A♭ Major	B♭ Major
					g Minor	A♭ Major	B♭ Major
C Major	D Major		E Major	F Major	G Major	A Major	B Major

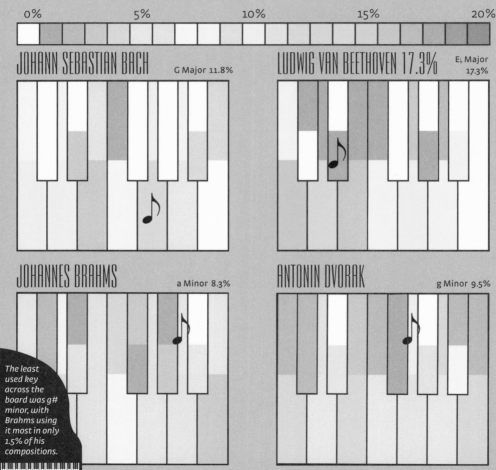

0%   5%   10%   15%   20%

JOHANN SEBASTIAN BACH   G Major 11.8%

LUDWIG VAN BEETHOVEN 17.3%   E♭ Major 17.3%

JOHANNES BRAHMS   a Minor 8.3%

ANTONIN DVORAK   g Minor 9.5%

The least used key across the board was g# minor, with Brahms using it most in only 1.5% of his compositions.

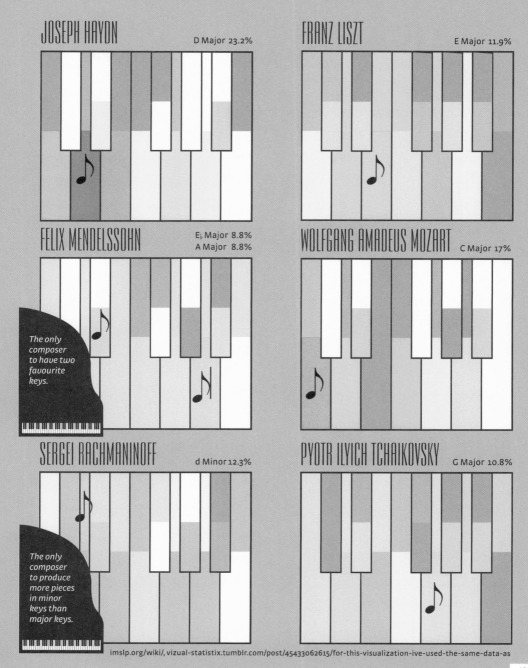

JOSEPH HAYDN — D Major 23.2%

FRANZ LISZT — E Major 11.9%

FELIX MENDELSSOHN — E♭ Major 8.8% / A Major 8.8%

The only composer to have two favourite keys.

WOLFGANG AMADEUS MOZART — C Major 17%

SERGEI RACHMANINOFF — d Minor 12.3%

The only composer to produce more pieces in minor keys than major keys.

PYOTR ILYICH TCHAIKOVSKY — G Major 10.8%

imslp.org/wiki/, vizual-statistix.tumblr.com/post/45433062615/for-this-visualization-ive-used-the-same-data-as

GET A **JOB**

Just like actors, wannabe rock stars usually start out working at regular jobs before they become famous. Here's what some world-famous rockers might have been earning if they'd stuck at the regular job and been promoted.

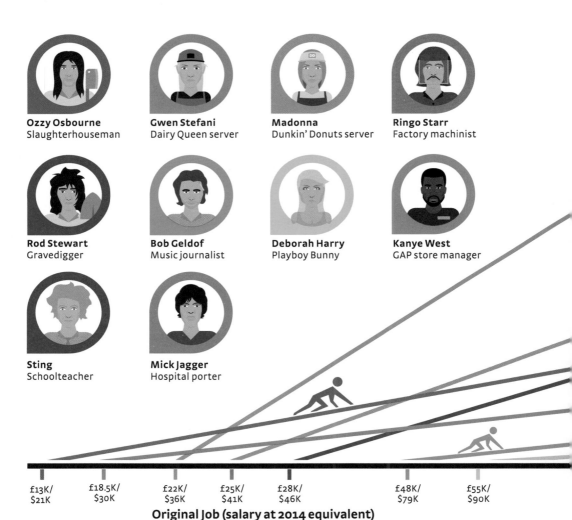

Ozzy Osbourne
Slaughterhouseman

Gwen Stefani
Dairy Queen server

Madonna
Dunkin' Donuts server

Ringo Starr
Factory machinist

Rod Stewart
Gravedigger

Bob Geldof
Music journalist

Deborah Harry
Playboy Bunny

Kanye West
GAP store manager

Sting
Schoolteacher

Mick Jagger
Hospital porter

£13K/
$21K

£18.5K/
$30K

£22K/
$36K

£25K/
$41K

£28K/
$46K

£48K/
$79K

£55K/
$90K

Original Job (salary at 2014 equivalent)

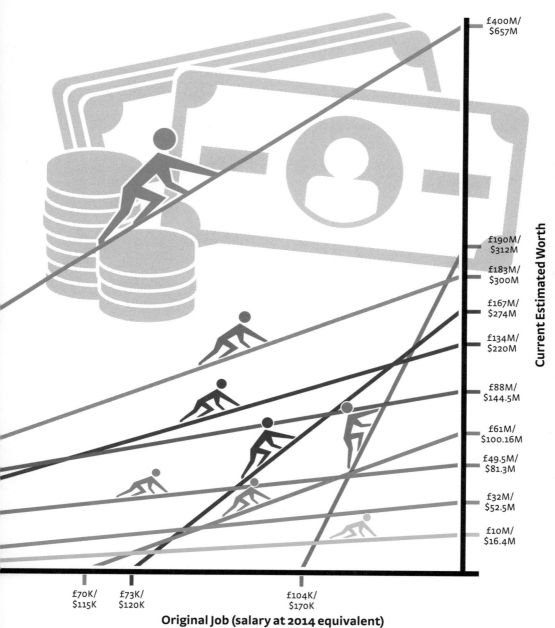

£400M/
$657M

£190M/
$312M

£183M/
$300M

£167M/
$274M

£134M/
$220M

£88M/
$144.5M

£61M/
$100.16M

£49.5M/
$81.3M

£32M/
$52.5M

£10M/
$16.4M

Current Estimated Worth

£70K/
$115K

£73K/
$120K

£104K/
$170K

Original Job (salary at 2014 equivalent)

wikipedia.org, celebritynetworth.com

45

NO ELVIS, BEATLES OR **STONES**

Since the turn of the century the way that music is consumed has changed radically, and so has the lineup of superstar performers who are the best-selling acts. Today, the former pop superstars of the 20th century are nowhere to be seen on post-millennium sales charts.

	ARTIST	COUNTRY	POPULATION
▶	**Britney Spears**	United States	317.0 million
▶	**Hikaru Utada**	Japan	126.5 million
▶	**Adele**	United Kingdom	63.0 million
▶	**Rammstein**	Germany	80.5 million
▶	**David Guetta**	France	66.0 million
▶	**Tiziano Ferro**	Italy	59.5 million
▶	**Shania Twain**	Canada	33.5 million
▶	**Delta Goodrem**	Australia	23.1 million
▶	**David Bisbal**	Spain	46.7 million
▶	**Andre Rieu**	Netherlands	16.8 million
▶	**Lasgo**	Belgium	11.0 million
▶	**Robyn**	Sweden	9.5 million
▶	**Show Luo**	China (Taiwan)	23.0 million
▶	**Faye Wong**	Hong Kong	7.0 million
▶	**Rihanna**	Barbados	0.284 million

RECORDS SOLD	TOTAL MUSIC PER COUNTRY (per million $)	AVERAGE SPEND PER PERSON	
▌▌▌▌▌▌▌▌▌▌	$ 4,481.80	BUY NOW	$ 14.13
▌▌▌▌▌	$ 4,422.00	BUY NOW	$ 34.95
▌▌▌▎	$ 1,325.80	BUY NOW	$ 21.04
▌▌▌	$ 1,297.90	BUY NOW	$ 16.12
▌▌	$ 907.60	BUY NOW	$ 13.75
▌	$ 217.50	BUY NOW	$ 3.65
▌▌▌▌▌▌▌▌▌	$ 453.50	BUY NOW	$ 13.53
▌▌	$ 507.40	BUY NOW	$ 21.96
▌	$ 166.60	BUY NOW	$ 3.56
▌▌▌	$ 216.30	BUY NOW	$ 12.87
▌	$ 121.50	BUY NOW	$ 11.04
▪	$ 176.70	BUY NOW	$ 18.61
▬	$ 56.00	BUY NOW	$ 2.43
▌	$ 37.00	BUY NOW	$ 5.25
▌▌▌▌▌▌▌▌▌▌▌▌▌▌	n/a	BUY NOW	n/a

Witchfinder General, Fates Warning, Possessed, Moonspell, Darkest Hour, White Zombie, Angel Witch, Burning Witch, Black Mass, Heathen Tomb, Coven, Pagan Altar, Pentagram, Stormwitch

Kiss, Cinderella, Twisted Sister, Girlschool, My Dying Bride, Satyricon, Vixen, White Sister

BLACK MAGIC

NASTY GIRLS

Black Sabbath, Judas Priest, Helloween, Death Angel, Candlemass, Cathedral, Sodom, Testament, Paradise Lost, Godflesh, Faith No More, Lamb of God, God Smack, God Forbid, Exodus, Meshuggah, St Vitus, Pantera, Sign Of The Beast, Babylon, Nazareth, Stryper

BIBLICAL EPICS

Metallica, Diamond Head, Tokyo Blade, Machine Head, Biohazard, Fear Factory, Tool, Rage Against The Machine, System Of A Down, Coal Chamber, Extreme Noise Terror, Anvil

HARD WORK

Repulsion, Unleashed, Anathema, Hatebreed, Mayhem, Enslaved, Disturbed, Savatage, Winger, Warrant, Korn, Prong, Borknagar, Overdose, Quireboys

SINGLE MINDED

Quiet Riot, Celtic Frost, Limp Bizkit, Guns N' Roses, Brutal Truth, Arch Enemy, In Flames, Shadows Fall, Suicidal Tendencies, Skid Row, Anal Apocalypse, Cradle Of Filth, Mercyful Fate, Metal Church, Hanoi Rocks, Primal Fear

THINGS THAT GO TOGETHER

NAME THAT **METAL**

When naming a heavy metal band most people have a common starting point, but there are some subtle and symbolic differences for different styles of metal that have to be decided upon. Gods or killers? Initials or one word? Ego or death?

ANIMALS
Steppenwolf, Scorpions, Whitesnake, Ratt, Therion, Wolfmother, Def Leppard, Bengal Tigers, Tygers of Pan Tang, Goatsnake, Black Widow, Iron Butterfly, Cancer Bats, British Lions, Mastodon, Raven, White Wolf, Wild Dogs

KILLERS
Cephalic Carnage, Slayer, Bathory, Dismember, Immolation, Killswitch Engage, Venom, Poison, Anthrax, Napalm Death, Stormtroopers Of Death, Nuclear Assault, Slipknot, Death From Above, Drowning Pool, Lawnmower Deth, Black Death, Killer Dwarfs

BIG THINGS
Led Zeppelin, Mountain, Europe, Megadeth, Nuclear Assault, Kreator, Destruction, Emperor, Aerosmith, Deth, The Darkness, Trouble

INITIALS
UFO, AC/DC, W.A.S.P., Static-X, Symphony-X, MGMT, +44, Kings-X, KMFDM, ZZ Top

GRAVE CONCERNS
Death, Morbid Angel, Dark Angel, Children Of Bodom, Overkill, Coroner, Autopsy, Type O Negative, Carcass, Grave, Entombed, Exhumed, Sepultura, Obituary, Sarcofago, At The Gates, Cannibal Corpse, Necrophobic, Dying Fetus, Dark Tranquility, Unearth, Gore Hearse, All That Remains, Gorefest, Funeral For A Friend

GODS AND WARRIORS
Saxon, Iron Maiden, Manowar, HammerFall, Hellhammer, Gogoroth, Darkthrone, Burzum, Deicide, Tiamat, Voivod, Chimaira, Dragonforce, Agathodaimon, Loki, Odin's Beard, Thor, Avenged Sevenfold

BLACK, BLUE AND PURPLE
Blue Cheer, Deep Purple, Blue Oyster Cult, Rainbow, Evergrey, Crimson Glory, Great White

GOTHIK
Dokken, Motörhead, Queensrÿche, Mötley Crüe, Dëthklok, Fœtus, Rammstein, Danzig

EGO
Dio, Van Halen, The Handsome Beasts, Michael Schenker Group, Marilyn Manson, Kid Rock

DEGREES OF SEPARATION
JOHN HIATT

You may not have heard of him, but John Hiatt has written hit songs for everyone from Bob Dylan to Paula Abdul, Buddy Guy, Jewel and Willie Nelson, plus many others. He's also released 21 rather fine studio albums.

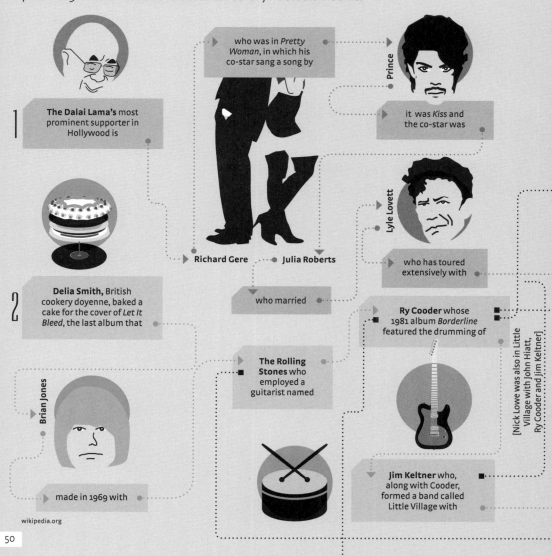

1 **The Dalai Lama's** most prominent supporter in Hollywood is

who was in *Pretty Woman*, in which his co-star sang a song by

Prince

it was *Kiss* and the co-star was

Richard Gere — **Julia Roberts**

Lyle Lovett

who has toured extensively with

2 **Delia Smith,** British cookery doyenne, baked a cake for the cover of *Let It Bleed*, the last album that

who married

Ry Cooder whose 1981 album *Borderline* featured the drumming of

The Rolling Stones who employed a guitarist named

[Nick Lowe was also in Little Village with John Hiatt, Ry Cooder and Jim Keltner]

Brian Jones

made in 1969 with

Jim Keltner who, along with Cooder, formed a band called Little Village with

wikipedia.org

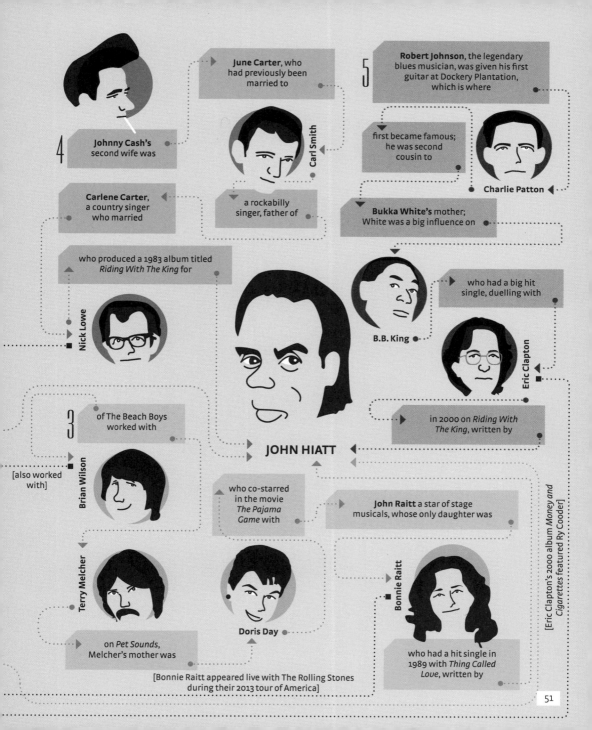

4 **Johnny Cash's** second wife was

June Carter, who had previously been married to

Carl Smith

a rockabilly singer, father of

Carlene Carter, a country singer who married

who produced a 1983 album titled *Riding With The King* for

Nick Lowe

5 **Robert Johnson**, the legendary blues musician, was given his first guitar at Dockery Plantation, which is where

first became famous; he was second cousin to

Charlie Patton

Bukka White's mother; White was a big influence on

B.B. King

who had a big hit single, duelling with

Eric Clapton

in 2000 on *Riding With The King*, written by

JOHN HIATT

3 of The Beach Boys worked with

Brian Wilson

[also worked with]

Terry Melcher

on *Pet Sounds*, Melcher's mother was

Doris Day

who co-starred in the movie *The Pajama Game* with

John Raitt a star of stage musicals, whose only daughter was

Bonnie Raitt

who had a hit single in 1989 with *Thing Called Love*, written by

[Eric Clapton's 2000 album *Money and Cigarettes* featured Ry Cooder]

[Bonnie Raitt appeared live with The Rolling Stones during their 2013 tour of America]

51

BOYS WILL BE GIRLS & GIRLS WILL BE BOYS

Detailing the major music acts who cross-dress and transgender musical artists of the past 50 years, there are 63 performers who deliberately confuse gender. Tracing their musical preference, rock and pop music are the major genres of choice.

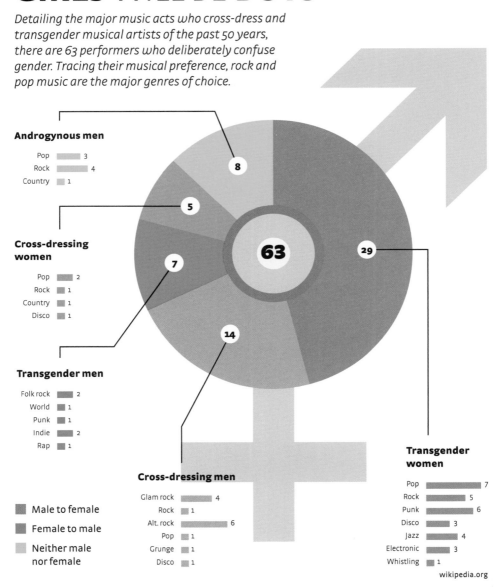

Androgynous men

Pop	3
Rock	4
Country	1

Cross-dressing women

Pop	2
Rock	1
Country	1
Disco	1

Transgender men

Folk rock	2
World	1
Punk	1
Indie	2
Rap	1

Cross-dressing men

Glam rock	4
Rock	1
Alt. rock	6
Pop	1
Grunge	1
Disco	1

Transgender women

Pop	7
Rock	5
Punk	6
Disco	3
Jazz	4
Electronic	3
Whistling	1

- Male to female
- Female to male
- Neither male nor female

wikipedia.org

52

MONSTERS OF ROCK (VARIOUS)
MOSCOW, RUSSIA
1991
1,600,000

PAUL VAN DYK, CARL COX, ARMIN VAN BUUREN (LOVE PARADE)
DORTMUND, GERMANY
2008
1,600,000

LOVE PARADE (VARIOUS)
BERLIN, GERMANY
1999
1,500,000

CONCERTO DEL PRIMO MAGGIO (VARIOUS)
ROME, ITALY
2006
2,350,000

PEACE WITHOUT BORDERS (VARIOUS)
HAVANA, CUBA 2009
1,500,000

JEAN MICHEL JARRE
PARIS, FRANCE
1990
2,500,000

THE ROLLING STONES
RIO DE JANEIRO, BRAZIL 2006
1,500,000

THE BIGGEST GIGS IN THE WORLD

The top ten live music concerts by attendances, the places where they occurred and when.

THE BEATLES
SHEA STADIUM, NEW YORK, USA
1965
56,600

JEAN MICHEL JARRE
MOSCOW, RUSSIA
1997
3,500,000

BABBU MAAN
DIRBA, INDIA
2008
4,080,000

ROD STEWART
RIO DE JANEIRO, BRAZIL
1994
3,500,000

RAPPERS **NOT DEAD**

Gangsta rap stars fill their songs with boasts about shooting and being shot, and often the claims are mere boasts. For these six stars the bullets were real but they lived to rap their tales.

TIMBALAND

Accidentally shot in kitchen by chef.

Recommended listening:
Tim's Bio: Life From Da Bassment, 1998

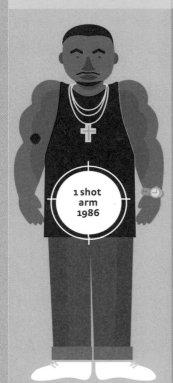

1 shot
arm
1986

GHOSTFACE KILLAH

Shot during an alcohol-induced altercation.

Recommended listening:
Bulletproof Wallets, 2001

1 shot
neck
early '90s

LIL WAYNE

Accidentally shot self aged 12.

Recommended listening:
Rebirth, 2010

1 shot
chest
1994

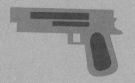

ODB *

Shot during an argument with another rapper. Shot during home invasion of girlfriend's apartment.

Recommended listening:
Return To The 36 Chambers, 1995
The Trials And Tribulations Of Russell Jones, 2002

LLOYD BANKS (G-UNIT)

Shot in a random act of violence.

Recommended listening:
Beg For Mercy, 2003

50 CENT

Shot in a car parked outside his grandmother's house.

Recommended listening:
Bulletproof, 2007

3 shots
stomach,
back, arm
1994/98

Died of a drug overdose in 2004.

2 shots
back,
stomach
2001

9 shots
arm, leg, hip,
chest, r-hand
2004

BEATS PER MINUTE

Disco conquered the world in the 1970s by setting a fairly scientific beats-per-minute ratio. Back then it was driven by a human drummer, but by 1993 BPM was set by machines on dance and club tracks. How much faster have we danced over the past 20 years, though?

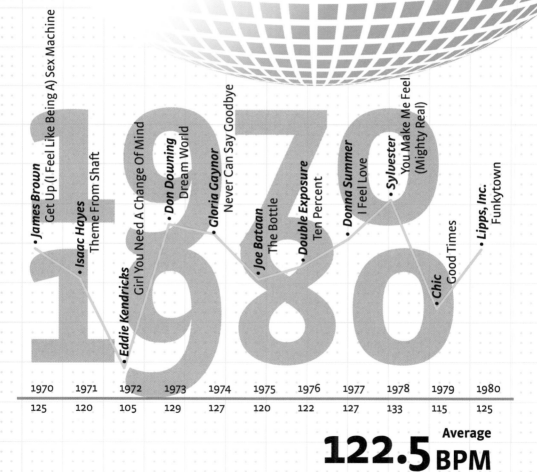

- *James Brown* Get Up (I Feel Like Being A) Sex Machine
- *Isaac Hayes* Theme From Shaft
- *Eddie Kendricks* Girl You Need A Change Of Mind
- *Don Downing* Dream World
- *Gloria Gaynor* Never Can Say Goodbye
- *Joe Bataan* The Bottle
- *Double Exposure* Ten Percent
- *Donna Summer* I Feel Love
- *Sylvester* You Make Me Feel (Mighty Real)
- *Chic* Good Times
- *Lipps, Inc.* Funkytown

1970	1971	1972	1973	1974	1975	1976	1977	1978	1979	1980
125	120	105	129	127	120	122	127	133	115	125

122.5 BPM **Average**

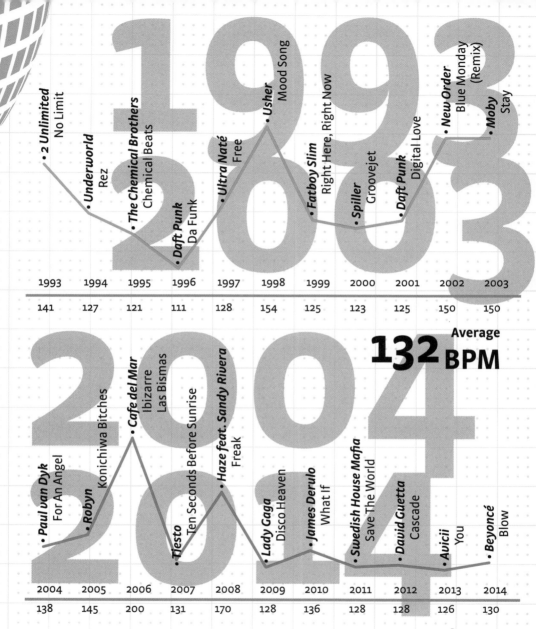

1993
2003

	1993	1994	1995	1996	1997	1998	1999	2000	2001	2002	2003
	141	127	121	111	128	154	125	123	125	150	150

- **2 Unlimited** No Limit
- **Underworld** Rez
- **The Chemical Brothers** Chemical Beats
- **Daft Punk** Da Funk
- **Ultra Naté** Free
- **Usher** Mood Song
- **Fatboy Slim** Right Here, Right Now
- **Spiller** Groovejet
- **Daft Punk** Digital Love
- **New Order** Blue Monday (Remix)
- **Moby** Stay

Average **132** BPM

2004
2014

	2004	2005	2006	2007	2008	2009	2010	2011	2012	2013	2014
	138	145	200	131	170	128	136	128	128	126	130

- **Paul van Dyk** For An Angel
- **Robyn** Konichiwa Bitches
- **Café del Mar** Ibizarre Las Bismas
- **Tiësto** Ten Seconds Before Sunrise
- **Haze feat. Sandy Rivera** Freak
- **Lady Gaga** Disco Heaven
- **James Derulo** What If
- **Swedish House Mafia** Save The World
- **David Guetta** Cascade
- **Avicii** You
- **Beyoncé** Blow

Average **142** BPM

songbpm.com, djbpmstudio.com

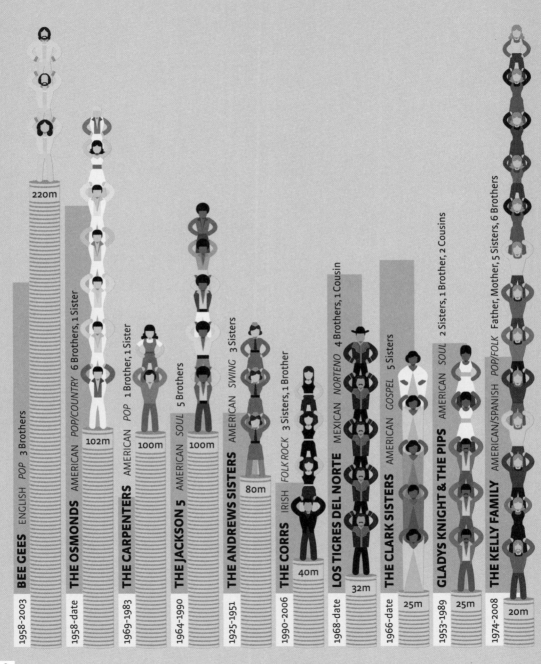

BEE GEES ENGLISH *POP* 3 Brothers
1958–2003
220m

THE OSMONDS AMERICAN *POP/COUNTRY* 6 Brothers, 1 Sister
1958–date
102m

THE CARPENTERS AMERICAN *POP* 1 Brother, 1 Sister
1969–1983
100m

THE JACKSON 5 AMERICAN *SOUL* 5 Brothers
1964–1990
100m

THE ANDREWS SISTERS AMERICAN *SWING* 3 Sisters
1925–1951
80m

THE CORRS IRISH *FOLK ROCK* 3 Sisters, 1 Brother
1990–2006
40m

LOS TIGRES DEL NORTE MEXICAN *NORTEÑO* 4 Brothers, 1 Cousin
1968–date
32m

THE CLARK SISTERS AMERICAN *GOSPEL* 5 Sisters
1966–date
25m

GLADYS KNIGHT & THE PIPS AMERICAN *SOUL* 2 Sisters, 1 Brother, 2 Cousins
1953–1989
25m

THE KELLY FAMILY AMERICAN/SPANISH *POP/FOLK* Father, Mother, 5 Sisters, 6 Brothers
1974–2008
20m

WE ARE **FAMILY**

The music biz has seen countless family member groups succeed over the years, but which ones were the most successful, and what familial relationship combination works best? Bands listed were originally comprised of family members only.

Active timeline

Sales

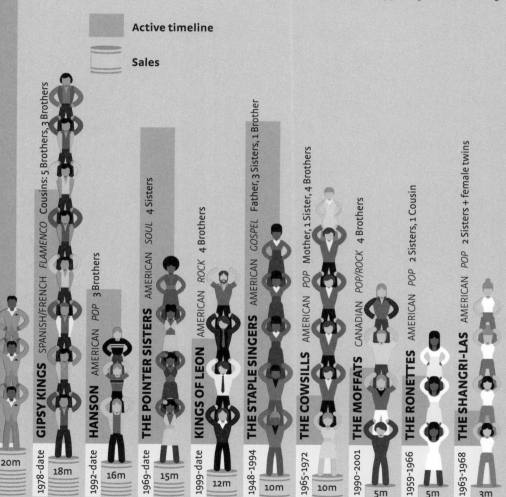

THE ISLEY BROTHERS AMERICAN *SOUL* 3 Brothers
1954–date 20m

GIPSY KINGS SPANISH/FRENCH *FLAMENCO* Cousins: 5 Brothers, 3 Brothers
1978–date 18m

HANSON AMERICAN *POP* 3 Brothers
1992–date 16m

THE POINTER SISTERS AMERICAN *SOUL* 4 Sisters
1969–date 15m

KINGS OF LEON AMERICAN *ROCK* 4 Brothers
1999–date 12m

THE STAPLE SINGERS AMERICAN *GOSPEL* Father, 3 Sisters, 1 Brother
1948–1994 10m

THE COWSILLS AMERICAN *POP* Mother, 1 Sister, 4 Brothers
1965–1972 10m

THE MOFFATS CANADIAN *POP/ROCK* 4 Brothers
1990–2001 5m

THE RONETTES AMERICAN *POP* 2 Sisters, 1 Cousin
1959–1966 5m

THE SHANGRI-LAS AMERICAN *POP* 2 Sisters + female twins
1963–1968 3m

wikipedia.org

59

HOW WE **LISTENED**

The story of recorded sound goes back to the middle of the 19th century and wax cylinders. Here are the leaps and bounds in technology that have driven the music business ever since.

1857

Wax cylinder recorder

Phonautograph, invented by Édouard Léon Scott de Martinville, records sounds onto wax cylinders

1948

12" vinyl 33 1/3rpm long player record

Columbia Records introduce the 12" vinyl 33 1/3rpm long player record

1935

AEG launch the K1 magnetic tape recorder (reel-to-reel)

1931

33 1/3rpm gramophone discs

RCA Victor introduce vinyl-made Victrolac discs that run at 33 1/3rpm

1930

Electrically powered phonogram

Electrically powered phonograms are launched

1949

7" 45rpm vinyl single disc

RCA Victor introduce the first 7" 45rpm vinyl single disc

1952

Dansette (UK) portable record player

The Dansette (UK) portable record player launched

1954

Transistor radio

The Regency TR-1 transistor radio is the first of its kind to be sold

1958

Stereo vinyl LP

Stereo vinyl LP records are introduced

2003

Uploading and streaming music launched

2001

Apple iPod

Apple iPod first generation 5GB MP3 player

1998

Portable MP3 player

HanGo Personal Jukebox launch first portable hard drive MP3 player from Compaq

1998

First MP3 player

SaeHan/Eiger MPMan launched as the first MP3 player

wikipedia.org, newworldrecords.com, electrotheremin.com, historyofrecording.com, indiana.edu/emusic, cec.sonus.com, richardhess.com

1877 **1896** **1897** **1898**

Tinfoil cylinder recorder

The tinfoil cylinder phonograph invented by Thomas Edison

Hand-cranked gramophone

A hand-cranked motorized gramophone is launched by Eldridge R. Johnson (USA) and Emile Berliner

First radio station

Guglielmo Marconi establishes first radio station on Isle of Wight, UK

First radio factory

Marconi opens the first wireless radio production factory in the world

1922 **1906** **1905** **1900**

First national radio company

The British Broadcasting Corporation becomes the first national broadcasting company via radio

First musical radio transmission

Reginald Fesenden (USA) makes first musical radio transmission on AM radio

78rpm-playing gramophone

The Victor Co launch The Victrola, a 78rpm-playing gramophone

First human voice transmitted by radio

Roberto Landell de Moura (BRA) sends first wirelessly transmitted human voice

1958 **1963** **1972** **1977**

8-track tapes

The magazine loading cartridge (8-track tapes) launched by RCA

Compact cassette

Philips (NETH) introduce the compact cassette player and tape

First 'music center'

Bang & Olufsen launch the Jacob Jensen-designed Beocenter containing vinyl record player, cassette deck and tuner amplifier

Stereobelt portable cassette player

Andreas Pavel launches the Stereobelt portable cassette player: it fails to catch on

1984 **1982** **1979**

Discman portable cd-player

Sony Discman D-50 portable cd-player launched

Compact Disc

The Compact Disc introduced by Sony (JPN) and Philips; first release was Billy Joel's 52nd Street

Sony Walkman

Sony Walkman portable cassette player launched

61

IT'S YOUR **FUNERAL**

And you can choose the music. You won't hear it, after all. Here are the most popular songs chosen for funeral services in the US, UK and Australia between 2005 and 2013. Points are awarded for the ranking of position in each of the seven charts used; the number of charts they appear in adds to the ranking.

Rank	Points	Charts	Song
1	43	6	My Way, Frank Sinatra
2	30	1	Angels, Robbie Williams
3	25	6	The Wind Beneath My Wings, Bette Midler
4	20	1	Somewhere Over The Rainbow, Judy Garland
5	17	4	Amazing Grace, Royal Scots Dragoon Guards
6	17	2	Time To Say Goodbye, Sarah Brightman & Andrea Bocelli
7	16	2	Stairway To Heaven, Led Zeppelin
8=8	14	2	Angel, Sara McLachlan
9	14	2	Goodbye My Lover, James Blunt
10	13	3	What A Wonderful World, Louis Armstrong
11	13	2	Good Riddance (Time Of Your Life), Green Day
12	11	3	Unforgettable, Nat 'King' Cole
13	11	2	Who Wants To Live Forever? Queen
14	10	1	Imagine, John Lennon
15=15	10	1	The Show Must Go On, Queen
16	9	2	Always Look On The Bright Side Of Life, Monty Python
	9	2	Tears In Heaven, Eric Clapton
	9	1	Hallelujah, Leonard Cohen

points

0
5
10
15
20
25
30
35
40
45

16 · 17=17 · 18 · 19=19 · 20=20 · 21=21 · 22 · 23=23 · 24=24 · 25=25 · 25=25

9 · 8 · 8 · 7 · 7 · 7 · 5 · 5 · 4 · 4 · 3 · 3 · 3 · 2 · 2 · 2 · 2 · 2 · 2

To Where You Are, Josh Groban

I've Had The Time Of My Life, Jennifer Warnes & Bill Medley

Highway To Hell, AC/DC

We'll Meet Again, Vera Lynn

Have I Told You Lately That I Love You? Van Morrison

I Will Remember You, Sara McLachlan

Candle In The Wind, Elton John

You Raise Me Up, Westlife

Everybody Hurts, REM

You'll Never Walk Alone, Gerry & The Pacemakers

I Will Always Love You, Whitney Houston

Let It Be, The Beatles

Live Forever, Oasis

Danny Boy, Daniel O'Donnell

Unchained Melody, The Righteous Brothers

Abide With Me, Harry Secombe

Every Breath You Take, The Police

My Heart Will Go On, Celine Dion

Nothing Else Matters, Metallica

points 0 · 5 · 10 · 15 · 20 · 25 · 30 · 35 · 40 · 45

points · #of charts · position

yourtribute.com, cooperative funeral services, Includeacharity.com, yahoo.com, European Music Census, Centennialpark.org

63

1967

Jimi's 'Guitar Burning' Outfit
Jimi Hendrix

Monterey Pop Festival

$49.99

1967

Sergeant Pepper Uniform
Paul McCartney

The Beatles – Hello, Goodbye music video

$32.99

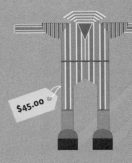

1972

Ziggy Stardust Space Suit
David Bowie

Ziggy Stardust tour

$45.00

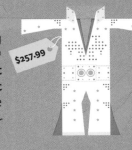

1973

American Eagle Jumpsuit
Elvis Presley

Aloha From Hawaii concert

$257.99

1975

Schoolboy Uniform
Angus Young

AC/DC stage outfit

$70 AUS

1976

Destroyer Costume
Gene Simmons

KISS stage outfit

$72.99

1977

White Dragon Suit
Jimmy Page

Led Zeppelin – North American tour

$N/A

1980

Rastafarian Satin Jacket
Bob Marley

Crystal Palace Concert Bowl

$32.99

Hollywoodtoysandcostumes.com, costumesupercenter.com, oceangrocecostumehire.com

1983
The Thriller Jacket
Michael Jackson
Thriller music video

$59.99

1984
Purple Rain Outfit
Prince
Purple Rain music video

$299.99

1985
Freddie's Wembley Costume
Freddie Mercury
Queen – Wembley Stadium Live Aid

$45.00

1986
Adidas Tracksuit
Run DMC
Raising Hell / My Adidas era

$38.00

1990
Hammer Pants
MC Hammer
U Can't Touch This music video

$40.99

1991
American Flag Bicycle Shorts
Axl Rose
Guns N' Roses stage outfit

$29.99

= price of costume hire

YOU WEAR IT **WELL**

Looking unforgettable has always been important in the music biz, and here are 14 iconic star outfits of the past 50 years. Plus, what it would cost to hire each of the costumes for one night only.

NEW WORLD MUSIC

Once upon a time, only Western pop music acts ruled the music markets on every continent. In the 21st century, though, the biggest-selling music acts of different nations are home-grown, and they outsell their Western counterparts.

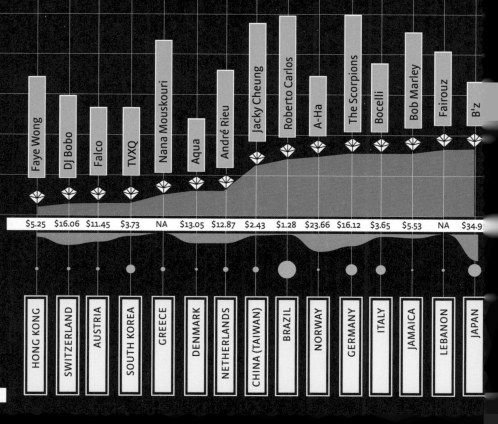

Faye Wong	DJ Bobo	Falco	TVXQ	Nana Mouskouri	Aqua	André Rieu	Jacky Cheung	Roberto Carlos	A-Ha	The Scorpions	Bocelli	Bob Marley	Fairouz	B'z
$5.25	$16.06	$11.45	$3.73	NA	$13.05	$12.87	$2.43	$1.28	$23.66	$16.12	$3.65	$5.53	NA	$34.9
HONG KONG	SWITZERLAND	AUSTRIA	SOUTH KOREA	GREECE	DENMARK	NETHERLANDS	CHINA (TAIWAN)	BRAZIL	NORWAY	GERMANY	ITALY	JAMAICA	LEBANON	JAPAN

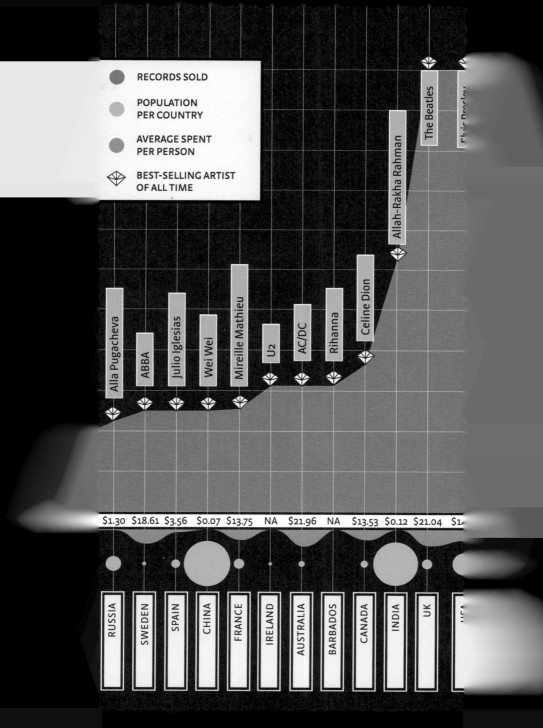

RECORDS SOLD

POPULATION PER COUNTRY

AVERAGE SPENT PER PERSON

BEST-SELLING ARTIST OF ALL TIME

Alla Pugacheva

ABBA

Julio Iglesias

Wei Wei

Mireille Mathieu

U2

AC/DC

Rihanna

Celine Dion

Allah-Rakha Rahman

The Beatles

RUSSIA	SWEDEN	SPAIN	CHINA	FRANCE	IRELAND	AUSTRALIA	BARBADOS	CANADA	INDIA	UK	
$1.30	$18.61	$3.56	$0.07	$13.75	NA	$21.96	NA	$13.53	$0.12	$21.04	$1...

FIDDLING **WHILE...**

*Solo instrumentals in the middle – or indeed throughout – a song
can often become tedious, even those played by Jimmy Page using a
violin bow. But they do allow the listener to go and do something else
instead. Here are a few suggestions of what to do during the solos.*

 Drums  Guitar  Bass guitar  Keyboards

	Moby Dick	Dazed & Confused	Sinister Minister	Maggot Brain	The Six Wives of Henry VIII
Soloist	John Bonham	Jimmy Page	Victor Wooten	Eddie Hazel	Rick Wakeman
Band	LED ZEPPELIN	LED ZEPPELIN	BÉLA FLECK & THE FLECKTONES	FUNKADELIC	YES
Date	1970	1977	1998	1971	1973
Length of solo	17.56	13.56	10.23	9.10	6.26
Other activity	Run 2 miles (3.2km) at **8mph (12.9kph)**	Helicopter over Victoria Falls **13m**	Clean out the refrigerator **10m**	Walk 790 yards (720m) at average speed **9m**	Fly from Connemara to Inishmaan Are Arann **6m**

68

Instrument	Date	Other activity

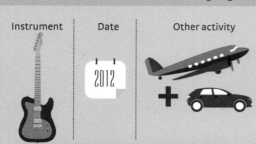

2012

Fly nonstop from Dubai to Houston (16hrs 20m, 13,144 km/8,168 miles) and drive nonstop from Houston to Clarksdale, Mississippi (8hrs 27m, 854.5 km/543 miles): **24hrs 47m, 13,998.5 km/8,711 miles**

Length of solo 24:55:00

	Freebird	War Pigs	Shine On You Crazy Diamond	Take A Pebble	Star Spangled Banner
Soloist	Rickey Medlocke	Tony Iommi	Dave Gilmour	Keith Emerson	Jimi Hendrix
Band	LYNYRD SKYNYRD	BLACK SABBATH	PINK FLOYD	EMERSON, LAKE & PALMER	-
Date	2010	1980	1974	1970	1969
Length of solo	6.08	5.50	5.17	4.55	3.57
Other activity	Iron three shirts **6m**	Cook an omelette **5m 30s**	Cook tuna and white bean crostino **4m 30s**	Boil an egg **3m 30s** & change a lightbulb **40s**	Pump 15.5 gallons of fuel **3m 57s**

Song title — Soloist — Band — Instrument — Date — Length of solo — Other activity

wikipedia.org, youtube.com, spotify.com

PAUL McCARTNEY

Hofner 'violin' bass custom made for Paul McCartney
$201,800 (£125,000), 2013

Paul McCartney's 1964 Aston Martin DB5
$568,000 (£344,440), 2012

$97k

GEORGE HARRISON

Leather jacket once belonging to George Harrison
$182,000 (£110,450), 2012

Gibson SG guitar, used by George Harrison to record Revolver LP
$567,000 (£343,740), 2004

Fender Telecaster guitar, Rosewood, used by George Harrison during the filming of Let It Be
$434,750 (£263,500), 2003

$567k

$201.8k

JOHN LENNON

Pair of round spectacles belonging to John Lennon
$97,000 (£58,000), 2009

John Lennon's Steinway Model Z piano sold to George Michael
$2.24m (£1.45m), 2000

John Lennon's tooth
$32,000 (£13,000), 2012

John Lennon's handwritten Bed Peace placard
$160,413 (£97,250), 2011

$32k

Most expensive item ever auctioned:
John Lennon's psychedelic Rolls-Royce Phantom V
$3.6m (£2.2m), 1985

RINGO STARR

Cape worn by Ringo Starr in the movie Help!
$37,500 (£22,500), 2011

Ringo Starr's Sgt Pepper's Lonely Hearts Club Band bass drum front
$893,000 (£541,250), 2008

THE BEATLES

$893k

$3.6m

Vox Custom prototype guitar owned by John Lennon and George Harrison
$408,000 (£247,000), 2013

Cardboard cutout of Marlene Dietrich, used on the cover of Sgt Pepper's Lonely Hearts Club Band LP
$142,000 (£86,250), 2003

CAN'T BUY ME **LOVE**

Rock auctions became a headline-grabbing business in the 1990s, and since then prices for the former belongings of certain musicians have increased enormously. If you're looking to start collecting, first find an artist who's dead, it seems, as this chart of the highest prices for items proves.

MICHAEL JACKSON

$49.9k

Jacket worn by Michael Jackson in Thriller video
$1.8m (£1.1m), 2011

Glove worn by Michael Jackson at the American Music Awards 1984
$196,800 (£117,900), 2011

Shirt worn by Michael Jackson in Scream video
$72,000 (£43,000), 2011

Fedora worn by Michael Jackson in Smooth Criminal video
$49,920 (£29,900), 2011

Wig belonging to Michael Jackson
$72,000 (£43,000), 2011

BOB DYLAN

$965k

Fender Stratocaster sunburst finish guitar, played by Bob Dylan at 1965 Newport Folk Festival
$965,000 (£585, 000), 2013

Signed Bob Dylan poster, inscribed with a poem to Elizabeth Taylor from Dylan
$80,500 (£48,200), 2011

$115k

$959k

ERIC CLAPTON

Fender Stratocaster 'Blackie' guitar owned by Eric Clapton
$959,000 (£581,000), 2004

Fender Stratocaster 'Brownie' guitar used by Eric Clapton to record Layla
$516,000 (£313,000), 1999

$46k

ELVIS PRESLEY

Nail Mirror jumpsuit worn on stage by Elvis Presley in 1973 and 1974
$175,000 (£104,800), 2006

Bespoke leather suit worn by Elvis Presley on stage in 1974
$120,000 (£72,000), 2008

Dark blue, sweat-stained International Continental suit worn by Elvis Presley on stage in 1975
$105,000 (£62,900), 2006

Elvis Presley's stage-worn and inscribed shoes
$46,875 (£28,000), 2013

Hair from Elvis Presley's head
$115,000 (£68,900), 2002

$300k

JUSTIN BIEBER

OZZY OSBOURNE

$40k

Hair from Justin Bieber's head
$40,688 (£24,300), 2011

$4.5k

Keys to Ozzy Osbourne's trashed quad bike
$4,500 (£2,700), 2003

JIMI HENDRIX

Jimi Hendrix's coat
$39,000 (£23,400), 2013

Fender Stratocaster guitar played by Jimi Hendrix at Woodstock Festival in 1969
$300,000 (£182,000), 1990

$957k

JERRY GARCIA

Custom-made 'Tiger' guitar owned by Jerry Garcia
$957,500 (£580,000), 2002

Custom-made 'Wolf' guitar owned by Jerry Garcia
$789,500 (£479,000), 2002

christies.com, bonhams.com, juliensauctions.com

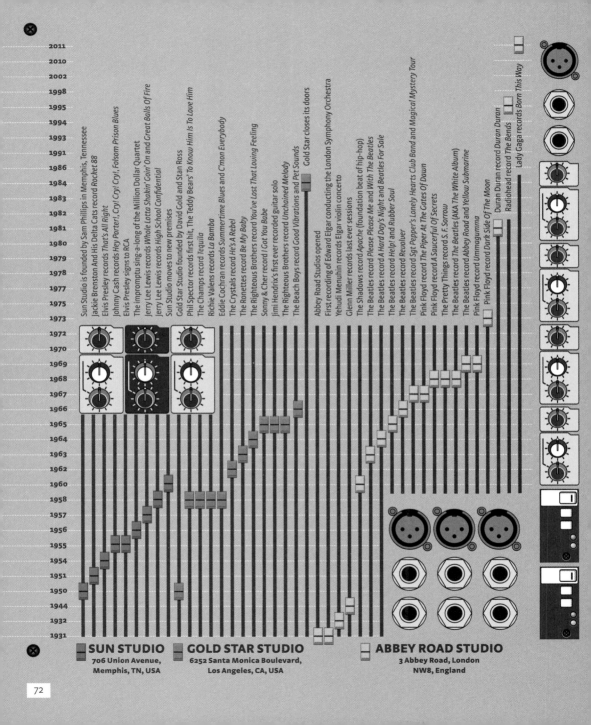

SUN STUDIO
706 Union Avenue, Memphis, TN, USA

GOLD STAR STUDIO
6252 Santa Monica Boulevard, Los Angeles, CA, USA

ABBEY ROAD STUDIO
3 Abbey Road, London NW8, England

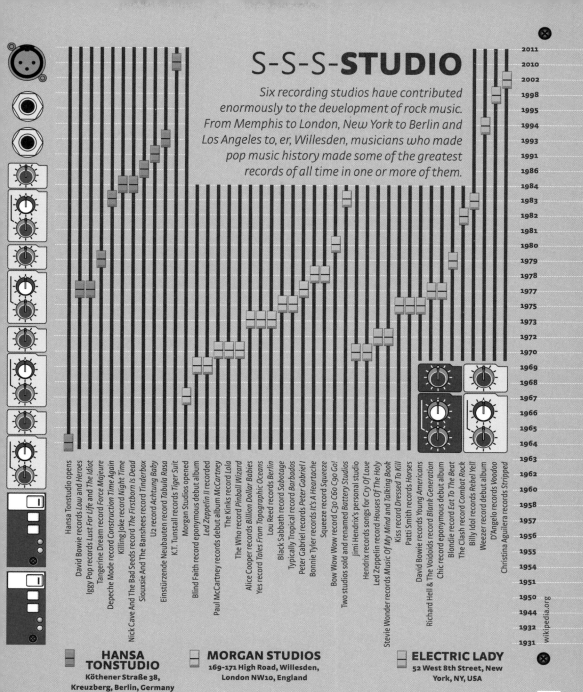

S-S-S-**STUDIO**

Six recording studios have contributed enormously to the development of rock music. From Memphis to London, New York to Berlin and Los Angeles to, er, Willesden, musicians who made pop music history made some of the greatest records of all time in one or more of them.

HANSA TONSTUDIO
Köthener Straße 38, Kreuzberg, Berlin, Germany

MORGAN STUDIOS
169-171 High Road, Willesden, London NW10, England

ELECTRIC LADY
52 West 8th Street, New York, NY, USA

wikipedia.org

Hansa Tonstudio opens
David Bowie records Low and Heroes
Iggy Pop records Lust For Life and The Idiot
Tangerine Dream record Force Majeure
Depeche Mode record Construction Time Again
Killing Joke record Night Time
Nick Cave And The Bad Seeds record The Firstborn Is Dead
Siouxsie And The Banshees record Tinderbox
U2 record Achtung Baby
Einstürzende Neubauten record Tabula Rasa
K.T. Tunstall records Tiger Suit
Morgan Studios opened
Blind Faith record eponymous debut album
Led Zeppelin II recorded
Paul McCartney records debut album McCartney
The Kinks record Lola
The Who record Pinball Wizard
Alice Cooper records Billion Dollar Babies
Yes record Tales From Topographic Oceans
Lou Reed records Berlin
Black Sabbath record Sabotage
Typically Tropical record Barbados
Peter Gabriel records Peter Gabriel I
Bonnie Tyler records It's A Heartache
Squeeze record Squeeze
Bow Wow Wow record C30 C60 C90 Go!
Two studios sold and renamed Battery Studios
Jimi Hendrix's personal studio
Hendrix records songs for Cry Of Love
Led Zeppelin record Houses Of The Holy
Stevie Wonder records Music Of My Mind and Talking Book
Kiss record Dressed To Kill
Patti Smith records Horses
David Bowie records Young Americans
Richard Hell & The Voidoids record Blank Generation
Chic record eponymous debut album
Blondie record Eat To The Beat
The Clash record Combat Rock
Billy Idol records Rebel Yell
Weezer record debut album
D'Angelo records Voodoo
Christina Aguilera records Stripped

2011
2010
2002
1998
1995
1994
1993
1991
1986
1984
1983
1982
1981
1980
1979
1978
1977
1975
1973
1972
1970
1969
1968
1967
1966
1965
1964
1963
1962
1960
1958
1957
1956
1955
1954
1951
1950
1944
1932
1931

WHAT'S IN A **NAME**?

Are the fashion for pop stars and baby names closely connected in celebrity-obsessed America? Here are a dozen hit songs and a dozen superstars, plus their name's position in the top 1000 baby names chart for every decade from the 1950s to the 2000s.

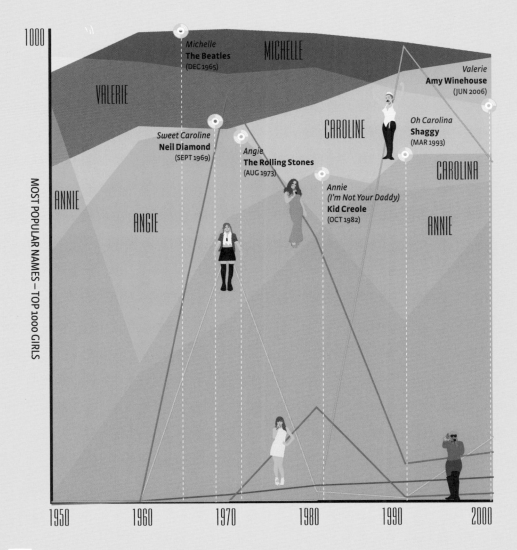

MOST POPULAR NAMES – TOP 1000 GIRLS

1000

Michelle
The Beatles
(DEC 1965)

MICHELLE

VALERIE

Valerie
Amy Winehouse
(JUN 2006)

Sweet Caroline
Neil Diamond
(SEPT 1969)

CAROLINE

Oh Carolina
Shaggy
(MAR 1993)

Angie
The Rolling Stones
(AUG 1973)

ANNIE

ANGIE

*Annie
(I'm Not Your Daddy)*
Kid Creole
(OCT 1982)

CAROLINA

ANNIE

1950   1960   1970   1980   1990   2000

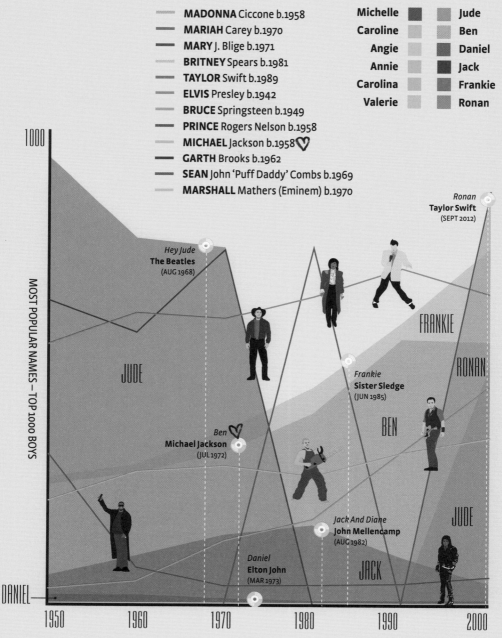

MADONNA Ciccone b.1958
MARIAH Carey b.1970
MARY J. Blige b.1971
BRITNEY Spears b.1981
TAYLOR Swift b.1989
ELVIS Presley b.1942
BRUCE Springsteen b.1949
PRINCE Rogers Nelson b.1958
MICHAEL Jackson b.1958
GARTH Brooks b.1962
SEAN John 'Puff Daddy' Combs b.1969
MARSHALL Mathers (Eminem) b.1970

Michelle   Jude
Caroline   Ben
Angie   Daniel
Annie   Jack
Carolina   Frankie
Valerie   Ronan

MOST POPULAR NAMES – TOP 1000 BOYS

1000

Ronan
Taylor Swift
(SEPT 2012)

Hey Jude
The Beatles
(AUG 1968)

FRANKIE

RONAN

JUDE

Frankie
Sister Sledge
(JUN 1985)

BEN

Ben
Michael Jackson
(JUL 1972)

JUDE

Jack And Diane
John Mellencamp
(AUG 1982)

Daniel
Elton John
(MAR 1973)

JACK

DANIEL

1950   1960   1970   1980   1990   2000

MUSICIANS WITH
DEGREES AND DOCTORATES

As Ian Dury once pertinently remarked, 'there ain't half been some clever bastards', possibly commenting on those who became musicians. But is there one type of music that attracts more musicians with degrees from notable universities than any other?

POP

Chris Martin
Coldplay
Degree: Ancient History, University College London

Will Champion
Coldplay
Degree: Anthropology, University College London

Jonny Buckland
Coldplay
Degree: Mathematics, University College London

Julio Iglesias
Singer
Degree: Law, Complutense University Madrid

Brian Briggs
Stornoway
PhD: Zoology, University of Oxford

Brian Cox
D:Ream
PhD: Physics, University of Manchester

Mira Aroyo
Ladytron
PhD: Molecular Genetics, University of Oxford

PUNK

Dexter
The Offspring
MD: Molecular Biology, University of Southern California

Greg Graffin
Bad Religion
PhD: Zoology, Cornell University

Milo Aukerman
The Descendents
PhD: Biochemistry, University of Wisconsin

Gregg Turner
Angry Samoans
PhD: Mathematics, Claremont University

Ethan Port
Savage Republic
PhD: Mathematics, University of Southern California

Dr James Lilja
The Offspring
MD: Gynecological Oncology, University of California

ELECTRONIC

Ben Gibbard
Postal Service
Degree: Environmental Chemistry, Western Washington University

Dan Snaith
Caribou
PhD: Mathematics, Imperial College

David Macklovitch
Chromeo
PhD: French Literature, Columbia University

Drew Daniel
Matmos
PhD: English Literature, University of California

FOLK

 Paul Simon
Degree: English, Queen's College

 Art Garfunkel
Degree: Mathematics, Columbia University

 Frank Turner
Degree: History, London School of Economics

OTHER

 Laurie Anderson
MD: Sculpture, Columbia University

Robert Leonard
Sha Na Na
PhD: Linguistics, Hofstra University

Buffy Sainte-Marie
Singer/Songwriter
PhD: Fine Art, University of Massachusetts

ROCK

 Richey Edwards
Manic Street Preachers
Degree: Political History, University of Wales

 Rivers Cuomo
Weezer
Degree: English, Harvard University

 Damian Kulash
Ok, Go
Degree: Art Semiotics, Brown University

 Tom Scholz
Boston
MD: Mechanical Engineering, Massachusetts Institute of Technology

 Brian Ferry
Roxy Music
Degree: Art, University of Newcastle

 John Perry Barlow
The Grateful Dead
Degree: Comparative Religions, Wesleyan University

 Jim Morrison
The Doors
Degree: Film, University of California

 Tom Morello
Rage Against The Machine
Degree: Political Science, Harvard University

 Thom Yorke
Radiohead
Degree: Art and Literature, University of Exeter

 Mark Knopfler
Dire Straits
Degree: English, University of Leeds

 Ezra Koenig
Vampire Weekend
Degree: English, Columbia University

 Matt Berninger
The National
Degree: Graphic Design, University of Cincinnati

 Kele Okereke
Bloc Party
Degree: English, King's College

 Brian May
Queen
PhD: Astrophysics, Imperial College

 Sterling Morrison
The Velvet Underground
PhD: Medieval Studies, University of Texas

 Phil Alvin
The Blasters
PhD: Mathematics & Artificial Intelligence, University of California

Warren Zanes
The Del Fuegos
PhD: Visual & Cultural Arts, University of Rochester

Music genre preferences for graduates

 P 17.5%   **Pu** 15%   **E** 10%   **F** 7.5%   **O** 7.5%   **R** 42.5%

wikipedia.org, music.cbc.com

A Audio
B Black
C Custom
D Damaged
E Electric
F Future
G Gold
H Honest
I Innocuous
J Juke
K King
L Lost
M Minor
N Northern
O Open
P Pacific

Q Quest
R Remote
S Static
T Temporary
U Unknown
V Vicious
W Wonder
X Xanthus
Y Yesterdays
Z Zero

THE FIRST WORD IS
the first letter of your mama's name

A Atlas
B Box
C Century
D Dreams
E Empire
F Flag
G Ghost
H Head
I Island
J Jam
K Kicks
L Legacy
M Music
N Nation
O Output
P Play

Q Quarter
R Restless
S Sound
T Takeover
U Union
V Victory
W Wave
X X-Ray
Y Youth
Z Zone

THE SECOND WORD IS
the first letter of your name

THE THIRD WORD IS
your birthdate

1 Android
2 Border
3 Cradle
4 Denial
5 Engine
6 Fast
7 Garage
8 Horny
9 Instant
10 Jury
11 Kaos
12 Lion
13 Master
14 Noonday
15 Outcast
16 Poorboys
17 Quorum
18 Road
19 Sinners
20 Truckers
21 Umbrella
22 Vice
23 Workers
24 XXX
25 Yen
26 Zap
27 Artists
28 Brothers
29 Sisters
30 Family
31 Gods

THE FOURTH WORD IS
this month

JAN Records
FEB Sounds
MAR Enterprises
APR Recordings
MAY Studios
JUN Limited
JUL Label Group
AUG Entertainment
SEPT Corp.
OCT Inc.
NOV Disques
DEC Discs

NAME YOUR RECORD **LABEL**

Now that the major labels are all but extinct and only signing acts who've been on a TV 'talent' show, worked with Swedish master mixers or are related/in a relationship with rappers-turned-businessmen, new talent might as well start their own 'label'. It'll need a name, and here's how to select one.

Beach Boys LPs 1962–2013

Studio 29	**Live** 5	**Compilation** 43
	Total songs recorded 412	

Beach Boys Greatest Hits ad nauseam
(songs released most times and on how many different LPs)

Good Vibrations	37
God Only Knows	33
California Girls	32
Sloop John B	30
I Get Around	30
Wouldn't It Be Nice	30
Heroes And Villains	29
Surfer Girl	27
Darlin'	27
Do It Again	27
Fun, Fun, Fun	26
Help Me, Rhonda	25
Barbara Ann	25
Little Deuce Coupe	24
Surfin' USA	23
Don't Worry Baby	23

BEACH BOYS RECORDINGS ABOUT

summer
(including surfing)
60

Christmas
21

vegetables
1

a day in the
life of a tree
1

a woman
going bald
1

THE WONDERFUL WORLD
OF **THE BEACH BOYS**

*In more than 50 years of recording together, America's former barber shop quartet
The Beach Boys have released over 400 songs on 77 albums. Some of the songs have
appeared on more than a few albums, as is shown here, along with other odd facts
about the band who were always about more than summer, surf and fun, fun, fun.*

Beach Boys LP covers featuring

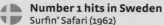

Beach Boys **25**

Number 1 hits in Sweden
Surfin' Safari (1962)
Little Honda (1964)
Sloop John B (1966)
Cottonfields (1970)

Number 1 hits in US
I Get Around (1964)
Help Me, Rhonda (1965)
Good Vibrations (1966)
Kokomo (1988)

waves / the sea **12**

cars **10**

surfboards **10**

cars and surfboards **2**

females **7**

a Native American on a horse **4**

cartoon flowers **3**

boats **2**

fish **2**

llamas **1**

Christmas trees **1**

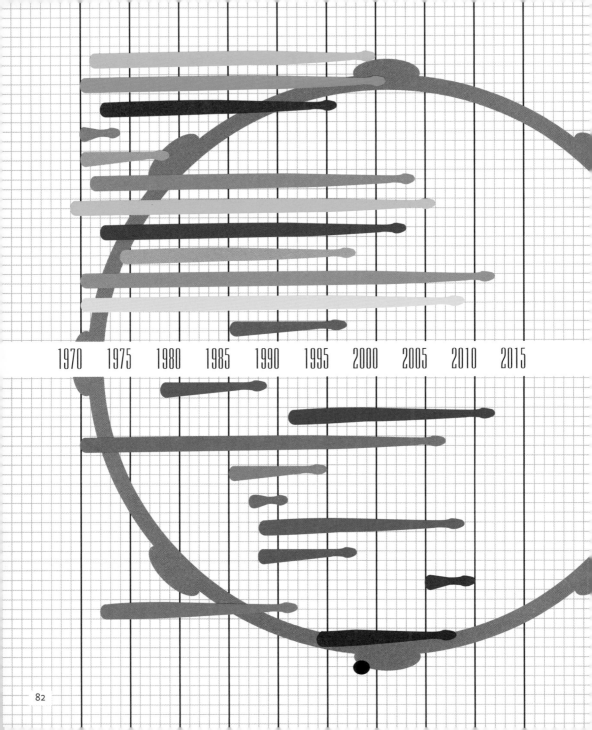

1970 1975 1980 1985 1990 1995 2000 2005 2010 2015

THE **PACEMAKER**

Drummer Jim Keltner is arguably the most connected drummer in the music business. He has worked with everyone, from Sun Records pioneers to blues legends, three-quarters of The Beatles to chief Pixie in the past 45 years. These are just the highlights of his career.

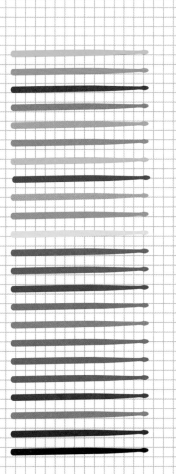

ARTIST'S NAME	NUMBER OF SONGS	DATE
Ry Cooder	14	1972–2001
George Harrison	11	1971–2002
Bob Dylan	10	1973–1997
John Lennon	7	1971–1975
Nilsson	7	1971–1980
Randy Newman	7	1972–2005
Joe Cocker	7	1970–2007
Ringo Starr	6	1973–2004
Dolly Parton	6	1975–1999
Carly Simon	5	1971–2013
Leon Russell	5	1971–2010
Elvis Costello	5	1986–1998
Tom Petty	5	1979–1990
T-Bone Burnett	5	1992–2013
B.B. King	4	1971–2008
Richard Thompson	4	1986–1996
Roy Orbison	4	1988–1992
Eric Clapton	4	1989–2010
David Crosby	3	1989–1999
Jerry Lee Lewis	3	2006–2011
Jackson Browne	3	1973–1993
Kris Kristofferson	3	1995–2009
Neil Young	3	1999–2000

jimkeltnerdiscography.blogspot.co.uk, wikipedia.org

🐐 AQUARIUS (1/20–2/18)

THE BRIGHT SIDE: Look at me! Look at me!
THE DARK SIDE: Who are you looking at?
THE ARTISTS: Eddie Van Halen, Justin Timberlake, Phil Collins, Alice Cooper, Bobby Brown, Bob Marley, Garth Brooks, Henry Rollins, Peter Gabriel, Axl Rose, Neil Diamond, Shakira, Harry Styles

🐟 PISCES (2/19–3/20)

THE BRIGHT SIDE: Want to teach the world to sing.
THE DARK SIDE: Sing my way, or get off my world.
THE ARTISTS: Rhianna, David Gilmour, Kurt Cobain, George Harrison, Johnny Cash, Tony Iommi, Jon Bon Jovi, James Taylor, Liza Minnelli, Nat 'King' Cole, Lou Reed, Justin Bieber

🐏 ARIES (3/21–4/20)

THE BRIGHT SIDE: Live life as only a diva can live.
THE DARK SIDE: Live life as only THIS diva can.
THE ARTISTS: Aretha Franklin, Elton John, Diana Ross, Steven Tyler, Mariah Carey, Celine Dion, Lady Gaga

🐂 TAURUS (4/21–5/20)

THE BRIGHT SIDE: We shall not be moved.
THE DARK SIDE: Full of bull.
THE ARTISTS: Pete Townshend, Bono, Willie Nelson, James Brown, Barbara Streisand, Tammy Wynette, Billy Joel, Stevie Wonder, Janet Jackson, Busta Rhymes

👯 GEMINI (5/21–6/21)

THE BRIGHT SIDE: Who am I today?
THE DARK SIDE: That wasn't me!
THE ARTISTS: Steve Vai, Chet Atkins, Prince, Bob Dylan, Paul McCartney, Morrissey, Miles Davis, Lenny Kravitz, Stevie Nicks, Gladys Knight, Alanis Morissette, Kenny G, Paula Abdul, Tom Jones, Tupac Shakur, Biggie Smalls

🦀 CANCER (6/22–7/22)

THE BRIGHT SIDE: In the mood for dancing.
THE DARK SIDE: In a mood.
THE ARTISTS: Joe Satriani, Carlos Santana, Yngwie Malmsteen, Al Di Meola, Beck, Cyndi Lauper, George Michael, Chris Isaak, Huey Lewis, Ringo Starr, Linda Ronstadt

BORN
UNDER
A **BAD
SIGN**

LEO (7/23–8/22) ♌

THE BRIGHT SIDE: I'll take care of this.
THE DARK SIDE: I SAID I'LL TAKE CARE OF IT!
THE ARTISTS: Jerry Garcia, Slash, Madonna, Mick Jagger, Whitney Houston, Kenny Rogers, Tori Amos

VIRGO (8/23–9/22) ♍

THE BRIGHT SIDE: Precision is all.
THE DARK SIDE: Control freak.
THE ARTISTS: Stevie Ray Vaughan, B.B. King, Nuno Bettencourt, Van Morrison, Joan Jett, LeAnn Rimes, Shania Twain, Gloria Estefan, Amy Winehouse, Elvis Costello, Michael Jackson, Barry White, Billy Ray Cyrus, Bruce Springsteen, Freddie Mercury, Leonard Cohen, Sean Combs aka P. Diddy, Beyoncé

LIBRA (9/23–10/22) ♎

THE BRIGHT SIDE: Loving, laughing, crying, singing.
THE DARK SIDE: What shall I be today?
THE ARTISTS: John Lennon, Trey Anastasio, Sting, Meat Loaf, Johnny Mathis, Paul Simon, Thom Yorke, Eminem, Jerry Lee Lewis, Snoop Dogg, Stevie Ray Vaughan, Tommy Lee, Toni Braxton, Julio Iglesias

SCORPIO (10/23–11/21) ♏

THE BRIGHT SIDE: Phoaaar!
THE DARK SIDE: Phew...
THE ARTISTS: Neil Young, Bonnie Raitt, Joni Mitchell, Björk, Bryan Adams, Anthony Kiedis, Ben Harper, Keith Urban, Art Garfunkel

SAGITTARIUS (11/22–12/21) ♐

THE BRIGHT SIDE: I'm an animal.
THE DARK SIDE: A chameleon.
THE ARTISTS: Jay-Z, Jimi Hendrix, Tom Waits, Ozzy Osbourne, Tina Turner, Bette Midler, Britney Spears, Sinead O'Connor, Frank Sinatra, Keith Richards, Edith Piaf, Nelly Furtado, Miley Cyrus

CAPRICORN (12/22–1/19) ♑

THE BRIGHT SIDE: Shy shy, too shy.
THE DARK SIDE: Meh.
THE ARTISTS: Jimmy Page, John McLaughlin, Zakk Wylde, Janis Joplin, Michael Stipe, Marilyn Manson, David Bowie, Elvis Presley, Pat Benatar, Rod Stewart, LL Cool J, Dolly Parton, John Denver, Aaliyah, Annie Lennox

Astrologers think they have us all summed up in their star-reading and rune-tumbling (don't they?). But does an astrological sign summation really apply to the world's biggest pop and rock stars?

wikipedia.org

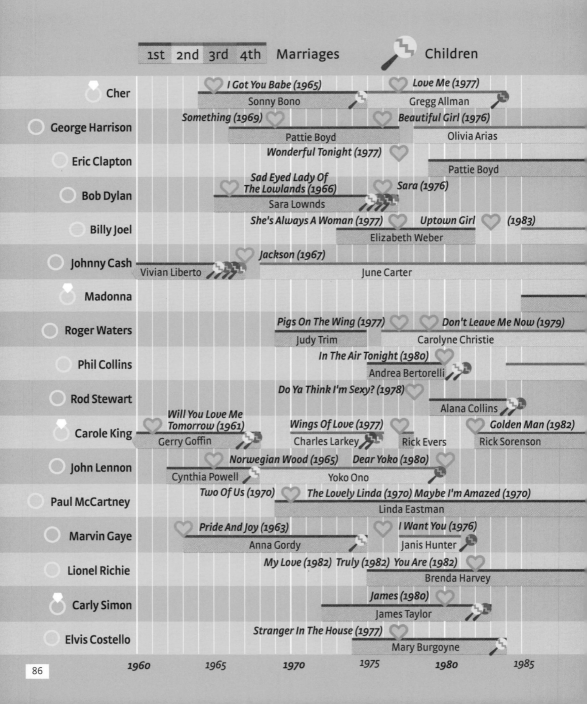

1st 2nd 3rd 4th Marriages   Children

Cher
I Got You Babe (1965)   Love Me (1977)
Sonny Bono   Gregg Allman

George Harrison
Something (1969)   Beautiful Girl (1976)
Pattie Boyd   Olivia Arias

Eric Clapton
Wonderful Tonight (1977)
Pattie Boyd

Bob Dylan
Sad Eyed Lady Of The Lowlands (1966)   Sara (1976)
Sara Lownds

Billy Joel
She's Always A Woman (1977)   Uptown Girl (1983)
Elizabeth Weber

Johnny Cash
Jackson (1967)
Vivian Liberto   June Carter

Madonna

Roger Waters
Pigs On The Wing (1977)   Don't Leave Me Now (1979)
Judy Trim   Carolyne Christie

Phil Collins
In The Air Tonight (1980)
Andrea Bertorelli

Rod Stewart
Do Ya Think I'm Sexy? (1978)
Alana Collins

Carole King
Will You Love Me Tomorrow (1961)   Wings Of Love (1977)   Golden Man (1982)
Gerry Goffin   Charles Larkey   Rick Evers   Rick Sorenson

John Lennon
Norwegian Wood (1965)   Dear Yoko (1980)
Cynthia Powell   Yoko Ono

Paul McCartney
Two Of Us (1970)   The Lovely Linda (1970)   Maybe I'm Amazed (1970)
Linda Eastman

Marvin Gaye
Pride And Joy (1963)   I Want You (1976)
Anna Gordy   Janis Hunter

Lionel Richie
My Love (1982)   Truly (1982)   You Are (1982)
Brenda Harvey

Carly Simon
James (1980)
James Taylor

Elvis Costello
Stranger In The House (1977)
Mary Burgoyne

1960   1965   1970   1975   1980   1985

I GOT **YOU** BABE

Musicians in love who get married often write and record songs about their spouses. There can be more than one song and more than one spouse, and they can say 'so long' as well as 'I love you'. As these many-times-married stars and their songs show.

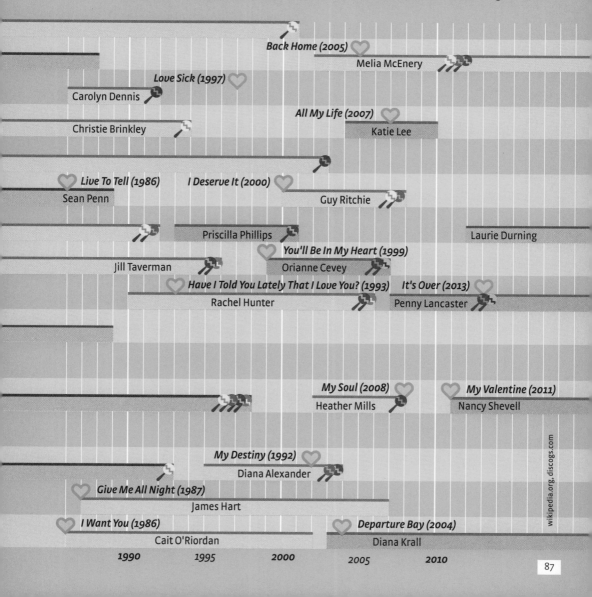

Back Home (2005) ♡
Melia McEnery

Love Sick (1997) ♡
Carolyn Dennis

All My Life (2007) ♡
Katie Lee

Christie Brinkley

Live To Tell (1986) ♡   *I Deserve It (2000)* ♡
Sean Penn   Guy Ritchie

Priscilla Phillips   Laurie Durning

You'll Be In My Heart (1999) ♡
Jill Taverman   Orianne Cevey

♡ *Have I Told You Lately That I Love You? (1993)*   *It's Over (2013)* ♡
Rachel Hunter   Penny Lancaster

My Soul (2008) ♡   *My Valentine (2011)* ♡
Heather Mills   Nancy Shevell

My Destiny (1992) ♡
Diana Alexander

♡ *Give Me All Night (1987)*
James Hart

♡ *I Want You (1986)*   ♡ *Departure Bay (2004)*
Cait O'Riordan   Diana Krall

1990   1995   2000   2005   2010

wikipedia.org, discogs.com

PROG ROCK **FREAK OUT**

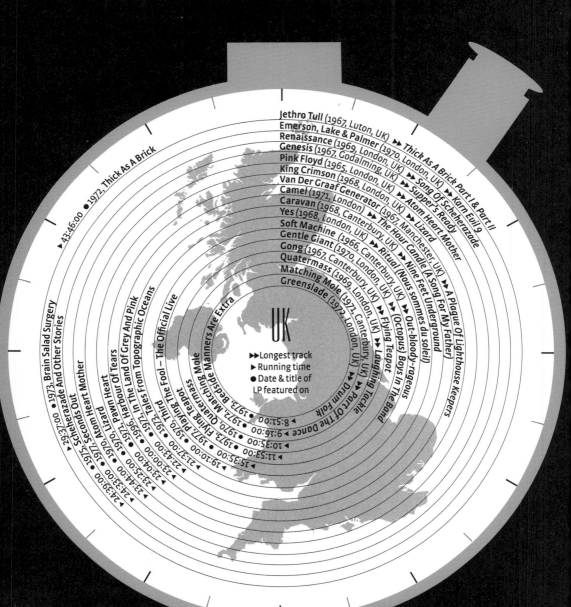

Jethro Tull (1967, Luton, UK) ▶▶ *Thick As A Brick Part I & Part II*
Emerson, Lake & Palmer (1970 London, UK) ▶▶ *Karn Evil 9*
Renaissance (1969, London, UK) ▶▶ *Song Of Scheherazade*
Genesis (1967, Godalming, UK) ▶▶ *Supper's Ready*
Pink Floyd (1965, London, UK) ▶▶ *Atom Heart Mother*
King Crimson (1968, London, UK) ▶▶ *Lizard*
Van Der Graaf Generator (1967 Manchester, UK) ▶▶ *The Hour Candle*
Camel (1971, London) ▶▶ *Nine Feet Underground*
Caravan (1968, Canterbury, UK) ▶▶ *A Plague Of Lighthouse Keepers*
Yes (1968, London, UK) ▶▶ *Ritual (Nous sommes du soleil)*
Soft Machine (1966, Canterbury, UK) ▶▶ *Out-bloody-rageous*
Gentle Giant (1970, London, UK) ▶▶ *(Octopus) Boys In The Band*
Gong (1967, Canterbury, UK) ▶▶ *Flying Teapot*
Quatermass (1969, London, UK) ▶▶ *Laughing Tackle*
Matching Mole (1971, Canterbury, UK) ▶▶ *Part Of The Dance*
Greenslade (1972, London, UK) ▶▶ *Drum folk*

UK

▶▶ Longest track
▶ Running time
● Date & title of
  LP featured on

▲ 43:46:00 ● 1972, Thick As A Brick

● 1973, Brain Salad Surgery
293:00 ● 1975, Scheherazade And Other Stories
● 1971, Seconds Out
● 1970, Atom Heart Mother
● 1972, Pawn Heart
● 1971, Harbour Of Tears
● 1996, In The Land Of Grey And Pink
● 1973, Tales From Topographic Oceans
● 1970, Third
● 1972, Playtime
● 1973, Flying Teapot
● 1970, Quatermass
● 1972, Matching Mole
● 1973, Bedside Manners Are Extra — The Official Live

24:39:00 ◀
24:33:00 ◀
23:44:00 ◀
23:00:00 ◀
22:43:00 ◀
21:37:00 ◀
19:10:00 ◀
15:35:00 ◀
11:53:00 ◀
10:35:00 ◀
9:16:00 ◀
8:51:00 ◀

Tracing the length of the longest vinyl-released single track by original progressive rock bands from Canterbury to Cologne, Uppsala to Luton, Milan to Paris, it appears that the Italians were less inclined to play longer tracks and 1973 was the prime year for freak outs.

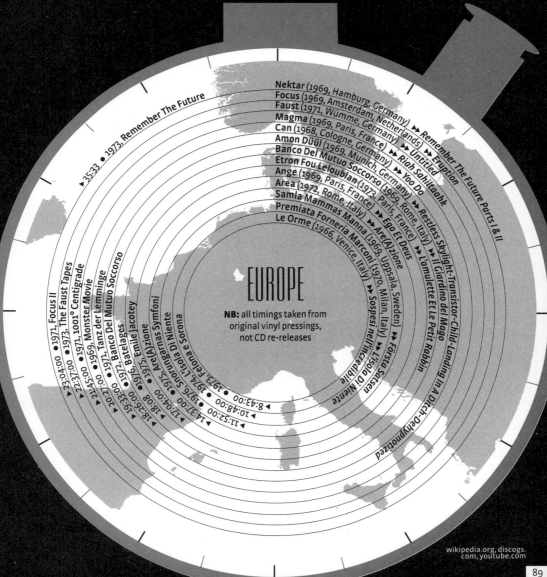

EUROPE

NB: all timings taken from original vinyl pressings, not CD re-releases

Nektar (1969, Hamburg, Germany) ▸▸ Remember The Future Parts I & II
Focus (1969, Amsterdam, Netherlands) ▸▸ Eruption
Faust (1971, Wümme, Germany) ▸▸ Untitled
Magma (1969, Paris, France) ▸▸ Riàh Sahìltaahk
Can (1968, Cologne, Germany) ▸▸ Yoo Doo
Amon Düül (1969, Munich, Germany) ▸▸ Restless Skylight-Transistor-Child-Landing In A Ditch-Derlyphonitzed
Banco Del Mutuo Soccorso (1969, Rome, Italy) ▸▸ Il Giardino del Mago
Etron Fou Leloublan (1973, Paris, France) ▸▸ Lamulette Et Le Petit Rabbin
Ange (1969, Paris, France) ▸▸ Are(A)zione
Area (1972, Rome, Italy) ▸▸ Ego Et Deus
Samla Mammas Manna (1969, Uppsala, Sweden) ▸▸ Första Såtzen
Premiata Forneria Marconi (1970, Milan, Italy) ▸▸ Sospesi nell'Incredibile
Le Orme (1966, Venice, Italy) ▸▸ L'Isola Di Niente

▸ 35:33 ● 1973, Remember The Future
▸ 23:04:00 ● 1971, Focus II
▸ 22:37:00 ● 1973, The Faust Tapes
▸ 21:45:00 ● 1971, 1001° Centigrade
▸ 20:27:00 ● 1969, Monster Movie
▸ 19:33:00 ● 1971, Tanz der Lemminge
▸ 18:26:00 ● 1972, Banco Del Mutuo Soccorso
▸ 18:08 ● 1976, Batelages
▸ 17:04:00 ● 1975, Emile Jacotey
▸ 14:37:00 ● 1975, Are(A)zione
▸ 11:52:00 ● 1976, Snorungarnas Symfoni
▸ 10:48:00 ● 1974, L'Isola Di Niente
▸ 8:43:00 ● 1973, Felona e Sorona

wikipedia.org, discogs.com, youtube.com

The Piper At The Gates Of Dawn
60,000 units

A Saucerful Of Secrets
60,000 units

More (Soundtrack)
100,000 units

Ummagumma
1.16 million units

Atom Heart Mother
1.35 million units

Meddle
2.4 million units

Obscured By Clouds
560,000 units

The Dark Side Of The Moon
50 million units

10,000

100,000

1,000,000

Units = total album sales

WHICH ONE'S **PINK?**

Pink Floyd revolutionized music when they emerged as a psychedelic rock four-piece in 1966. With every album release from 1967 to 1973 their sales increased incredibly, and while it slackened a bit after they'd been to the Dark Side Of The Moon, they still enjoyed enormous success as this timeline shows.

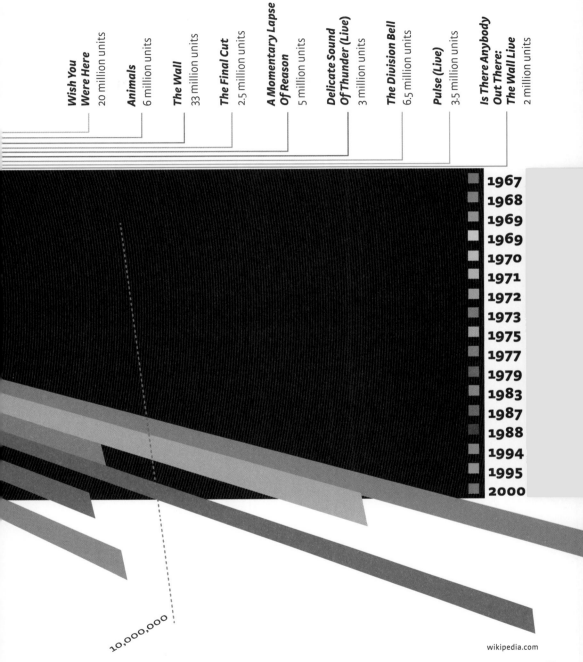

Wish You Were Here
20 million units

Animals
6 million units

The Wall
33 million units

The Final Cut
2.5 million units

A Momentary Lapse Of Reason
5 million units

Delicate Sound Of Thunder (Live)
3 million units

The Division Bell
6.5 million units

Pulse (Live)
3.5 million units

Is There Anybody Out There: The Wall Live
2 million units

1967
1968
1969
1969
1970
1971
1972
1973
1975
1977
1979
1983
1987
1988
1994
1995
2000

10,000,000

SPLIT **TICKET**

The costs of touring for an artist of any size has to be recouped from the ticket price.
But not every act can make money out of ticket sales alone, as this breakdown of
costs for one gig by Fish and his band at a medium-sized venue in Europe, shows.

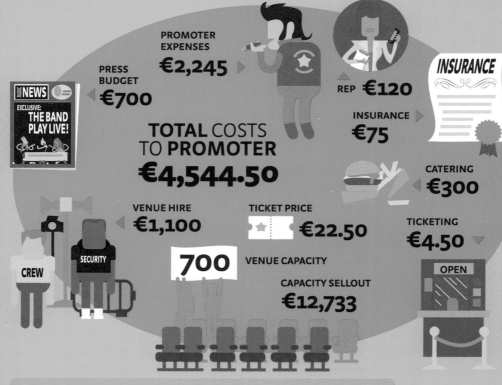

**PROMOTER
EXPENSES**

€2,245

**PRESS
BUDGET**

€700

MUSIC **NEWS**

EXCLUSIVE:
**THE BAND
PLAY LIVE!**

REP **€120**

INSURANCE

INSURANCE

€75

TOTAL COSTS
TO **PROMOTER**

€4,544.50

CATERING

€300

VENUE HIRE

€1,100

TICKET PRICE

€22.50

TICKETING

€4.50

700 **VENUE CAPACITY**

SECURITY

CREW

CAPACITY SELLOUT

€12,733

OPEN

POINTS TO NOTE

Guarantee (beyond which the share in profits is split 70:30 in favour of the artist):
€2,250 or 273 tickets.

The above figures would net a €246 loss against the guarantee,
but with merchandising that's converted to a €254 profit.

For each 100 tickets sold above the guarantee, the artist stands to make
€1,200+ additional merchandise revenue.

However, sales rarely exceed 500 tickets per gig.

On a 12-date tour with 3 off-days, the net loss if merchandising is not factored in is €6,500.

A sellout tour of this type would gross €45,000, less taxes, but that would be unusual.

GUARANTEE

€2,250

— OR —

273

TICKETS

SPLITTER VAN HIRE **€110** ▲

CREW WAGES
€400

FUEL
€72 ▶

TOURING AGENCY FEE
€113

MERCHANDISING
FACILITY FEE
€50 ▼

HOTEL **€400** ▲

REHEARSALS
€416

STRINGS,
SKINS, ETC
€42

INSURANCE

TOTAL COSTS
TO PERFORMER
€2,495.00

INSURANCE
€42

BREAKFAST
€25 ▲

VIDEO HIRE
€75

BAND'S WAGES
€750

LOVE TO LOVE YOU BABY

In the 1960s the rock 'n' roll world was remarkably small, and everybody who was anybody knew each other. They played the same gigs, used the same studios and made love, not war, with each other. At the heart of the interconnectivity were men and women who just seemed to love too much.

Crosby and Nash's bandmate **Stephen Stills**

Rita left Stills for Nash

fell in love with **Rita Coolidge**

who had recently left

JONI MITCHELL

GRAHAM NASH

who had signed a recording contract with **David Geffen**

who went on to marry **Kris Kristofferson**

who had earlier had an affair with **Joan Baez**

who met Joni via her lover **David Crosby**

a lover of **Cher**

a former lover of

a few weeks after her brief affair with

who had been married to **Sonny Bono**

LEONARD COHEN

who was in a relationship with

BOB DYLAN

who was on tour with **Sam Shepard**

and then **Gregg Allman**

Nash had written the song *Carrie Ann* for Marianne

who had a fling with **Marianne Faithfull** who had been Mick's partner until the early 1970s when

The Rolling Stones' **Brian Jones**

had an affair with **Carly Simon**

dated **Anita Pallenberg** until she left him for

who was engaged to **James Taylor** at the time, and who was friends with

MICK JAGGER

KEITH RICHARDS

and had a daughter **Mackenzie** who later had a fling with

was married to **Bianca Jagger**

played Anita Pallenberg's lover in the 1970 movie *Performance* which annoyed

who was married to **Michelle Phillips** at the time

when he met **Jerry Hall** via her lover

Michelle was married to *Dennis Hopper* for eight days

BRYAN FERRY

who previously had an affair with **John Phillips**

CARLY SIMON

she then met **Warren Beatty** who'd had an affair with

having met him via lover **Gene Clark**

HOW TO **MAKE IT** IN THE MUSIC BIZ

The music business changed enormously between the mid-1990s and 2014, and not only in the way that music is consumed. Ways of making music and making it in the business have also undergone some radical changes. Here's how.

MAKING IT IN 2014

b. 1997

Age 4–10 (2001–2007) Learn to play Gameboy, PS2, PS3, Wii • Practise for 10,000 hours • Discover MySpace ★ **Age 10–13 (2007–2010)** Get seriously into YouTube • Upload videos of self singing along to mum's fave music • Start a MySpace page and upload three sing-along tracks • Get family and friends to 'like' all videos and Facebook page • Get local newspaper to run a story about how many thousands of online fans you have • Learn to sing a power ballad with lots of vibrato in the voice • Audition for major TV talent show, get rejected for being too young ★ **Age 13–15 (2010–2012)** Buy an Apple laptop with Pro Tools and Auto-Tune • Take a star-making course, get the owner to manage your career • Meet older boys who know how to lay down tracks • Subscribe to a beats stream • Create new tunes out of fave old ones in your bedroom • Audition for X Factor • Get onto X Factor ★ **PROFESSIONAL STEPS** • **Years 1–2 (2012–2013)** Do well enough on X Factor to be offered a professional contract with Syco or similar production company • Get a make-over • Put vocals on tracks chosen by production company • Duet with Gary Barlow or Will.i.am • Release a single online only, and every hour for the following 24 release a new mix of the same single • Give your heartbreaking story exclusively to a major daily newspaper or glossy magazine • Production company will send the story and single viral • The release becomes 'the fastest-selling debut single this century'™ (in Latvia) • Begin the X Factor live tour and leave after three appearances due to musical differences ★ **Year 3 (2014)** Date a major Hollywood star, internationally recognized sportsperson or slightly older major pop star • Sing guest vocals on a production by Max Martin, RedOne or David Guetta • Become the face or body of a revitalized clothing brand • Arrange to be seen on stage with Madonna • Put vocals on top of a pre-made bunch of songs that will be released as the debut album, at a rate of one track a month • Be paid to appear on a celebrity reality TV show

YOU'VE MADE IT

AND IN
THE END

The Beatles were the most successful recording group in pop music history. When they split up in 1970 each began a solo recording career. While Paul has persisted in making music and by sheer weight of numbers sold more albums than the other former Fabs, they have done surprisingly well. Ringo is the only one to appear on solo releases by all of his former bandmates. The lists do not include compilation albums nor those on which they make only guest appearances.

Give My Regards To Broad Street (1984) + Ringo **1 M**

Pipes Of Peace (1983) + Ringo **1.6 M**

Tug Of War (1982) + Ringo **1.25 M**

The Traveling Wilburys Vol. 3 (1990) **1.4 M**

The Traveling Wilburys Vol. 1 (1988) **3.66 M**

Cloud Nine (1987) **1.6 M**

All Things Must Pass (1970) + Ringo **6.1 M**

LIFETIME EARNINGS

$ 16.83 M

$ 29.33 M

$ 5.39 M

$ 9.65 M

GEORGE

PAUL

RINGO

JOHN

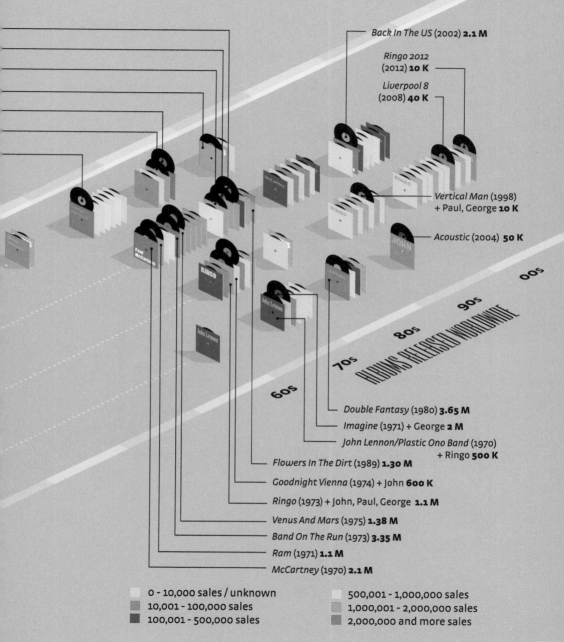

Back In The US (2002) **2.1 M**

Ringo 2012
(2012) **10 K**

Liverpool 8
(2008) **40 K**

Vertical Man (1998)
+ Paul, George **10 K**

Acoustic (2004) **50 K**

ALBUMS RELEASED WORLDWIDE

60s 70s 80s 90s 00s

Double Fantasy (1980) **3.65 M**
Imagine (1971) + George **2 M**
John Lennon/Plastic Ono Band (1970)
+ Ringo **500 K**
Flowers In The Dirt (1989) **1.30 M**
Goodnight Vienna (1974) + John **600 K**
Ringo (1973) + John, Paul, George **1.1 M**
Venus And Mars (1975) **1.38 M**
Band On The Run (1973) **3.35 M**
Ram (1971) **1.1 M**
McCartney (1970) **2.1 M**

0 - 10,000 sales / unknown
10,001 - 100,000 sales
100,001 - 500,000 sales

500,001 - 1,000,000 sales
1,000,001 - 2,000,000 sales
2,000,000 and more sales

RADIOHEAD SONGS BY GENRE

How to correctly file Radiohead tracks in your MP3 library.

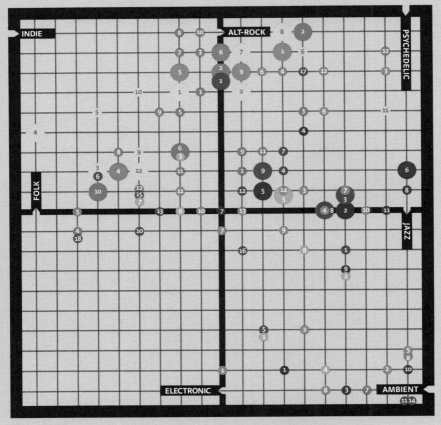

PABLO HONEY: 1 YOU 2 CREEP 3 HOW DO YOU? 4 STOP WHISPERING 5 THINKING ABOUT YOU
6 ANYONE CAN PLAY GUITAR 7 RIPCORD 8 VEGETABLE 9 PROVE YOURSELF 10 I CAN'T 11 LURGEE 12 BLOW OUT

THE BENDS: 1 PLANET TELEX 2 THE BENDS 3 HIGH AND DRY 4 FAKE PLASTIC TREES 5 BONES 6 (NICE DREAM) 7 JUST
8 MY IRON LUNG 9 BULLET PROOF... I WISH I WAS 10 BLACK STAR 11 SULK 12 STREET SPIRIT (FADE OUT)

OK COMPUTER: 1 AIRBAG 2 PARANOID ANDROID 3 SUBTERRANEAN HOMESICK ALIEN 4 EXIT MUSIC (FOR A FILM) 5 LET DOWN
6 KARMA POLICE 7 FITTER HAPPIER 8 ELECTIONEERING 9 CLIMBING UP THE WALLS 10 NO SURPRISES 11 LUCKY 12 THE TOURIST

KID A: 1 EVERYTHING IN ITS RIGHT PLACE 2 KID A 3 THE NATIONAL ANTHEM 4 HOW TO DISAPPEAR COMPLETELY
5 TREEFINGERS 6 OPTIMISTIC 7 IN LIMBO 8 IDIOTEQUE 9 MORNING BELL 10 MOTION PICTURE SOUNDTRACK

AMNESIAC: 1 PACKT LIKE SARDINES IN A CRUSHD TIN BOX 2 PYRAMID SONG 3 PULK/PULL REVOLVING DOORS 4 YOU AND WHOSE ARMY 5 I MIGHT
BE WRONG 6 KNIVES OUT 7 MORNING BELL/AMNESIAC 8 DOLLARS & CENTS 9 HUNTING BEARS 10 LIKE SPINNING PLATES 11 LIFE IN A GLASSHOUSE

HAIL TO THE THIEF: 1 2+2 = 5 2 SIT DOWN STAND UP 3 SAIL TO THE MOON 4 BACKDRIFTS 5 GO TO SLEEP 6 WHERE I END YOU BEGIN 7 WE SUCK YOUNG
BLOOD 8 THE GLOAMING 9 THERE THERE 10 I WILL 11 A PUNCH UP AT A WEDDING 12 MYXOMATOSIS 13 SCATTERBRAIN 14 A WOLF AT THE DOOR

IN RAINBOWS: 1 15 STEP 2 BODYSNATCHERS 3 NUDE 4 WEIRD FISHES/ARPEGGI 5 ALL I NEED 6 FAUST ARP 7 RECKONER 8 HOUSE OF CARDS
9 JIGSAW FALLING INTO PLACE 10 VIDEOTAPE **BONUS DISK 11 MK1 12 DOWN IS THE NEW UP 13 GO SLOWLY 14 MK2 15 LAST FLOWERS
16 UPON THE LATTER 17 BANGERS & MASH 18 4 MINUTE WARNING

THE KING OF LIMBS: 1 BLOOM 2 MORNING MR MAGPIE 3 LITTLE BY LITTLE 4 FERAL 5 LOTUS FLOWER 6 CODEX 7 GIVE UP THE GHOST
8 SEPARATOR

cargocollective.com/jamiegurnell/Radiohead-A-Genre

MUSIC SALES
BY GENRE

The dots denote whether the statistic is European (black dots) or American (grey dots). The sound of music is not, it seems, appreciated in equal measure by Americans and Europeans. Sales of different music by genre on each continent demonstrates the cultural and musical differences between the two. While rock music accounts for a large percentage of sales everywhere, Americans buy more metal than in Europe, where buyers prefer dance.

Easy listening 7.9%

Country 11.3%

Rock 28.4%

R&B 13.5%

Dance 7.1%

Rock 29.4%

Dance 5.8%

Pop 25.6%

Classical 3.6%

Religious 2.5%

Folk 1.6%

R&B 20.6%

Jazz 1.3%

Classical 1.3%

Country 1%

Holiday 1.1%

Blues 0.9%

Blues 0.2%

World 0.5%

Jazz 0.7%

Reggae 0.5%

Pop 33.6%

Children's 0.3%

Comedy 0.5%

New age 0.1%

World 0.3%

New age 0.1%

Children's 0.3%

Europe

United States

wikipedia.org

101

Miles Davis (1926–1991) first self-written album was *Kind Of Blue*, 1959 [it is now the biggest-selling jazz album of all time, ₤om+ units].

Miles Davis covered more songs written by George and Ira Gershwin (15) and Richard Rodgers (6) than any other writers.

Thelonius Monk (1917–1982) first self-written album was *5 By Monk 5* (1959). He performed with Miles Davis on two albums (1954) and with John Coltrane on two live recordings (1957).

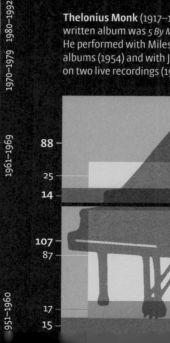

1980–1992

1970–1979

1961–1969

951–1960

88

25

14

107
87

17
15

■ *LPs*
■ *total number songs*
   out of which
   ■ *# original compositions*
   ■ *# showtunes*

Ornette Coleman (1930–) first self-
penned album was *Something Else!!!!* (1958),
his debut release.

The only showtune covered by **Coleman**
was written by George and Ira Gershwin,
Embraceable You (in 1959).

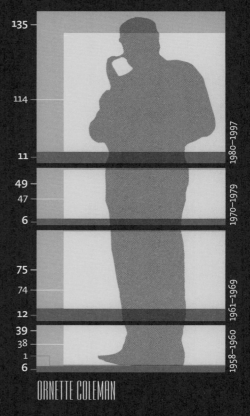

John Coltrane (1926–1964) first self-
written album was *Giant Steps* (1960).
Coltrane appeared on 11 of Miles
Davis' albums (1955–1961).

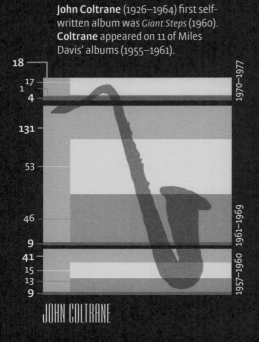

JOHN COLTRANE

ORNETTE COLEMAN

www.jazzstandards.com, www.allmusic.com, www.wikipedia.org

HOW MANY BOYS
MAKE A BAND?

The Beatles set the bar for subsequent boy bands and The Monkees were the first attempt to emulate the Fab Four's success; One Direction are the latest 'new Beatles'. But how many songwriters, musicians and producers does it take to be the #1 boy band in the world?

Year	1960	'63	'63	'64	'64	'65	'65	'66	'66	'67	'67	'67	'67	'67	'68	'68	'68	'69	'69	'69
Albums		Please Please Me	With The Beatles	A Hard Day's Night	Beatles For Sale	Help!	Rubber Soul	Revolver	The Monkees	Sgt Pepper's Lonely Hearts Club Band	Magical Mystery Tour	More Of The Monkees	Headquarters	Pisces, Aquarius, Capricorn & Jones Ltd.	The Beatles	The Birds, The Bees And The Monkees	Head	Abbey Road	Instant Replay	The Monkees Present
Tracks		14	14	13	14	14	14	14	12	13	11	12	14	13	30	12	14	17	12	12
Songwriters excluding band		12	11	0	7	3	0	0	7	0	0	19	13	17	0	13	6	0	8	7
									Plus Michael Nesmith			Plus Michael Nesmith	Plus all four of the group	Plus three of the group		Plus two of the group	Plus two of the group		Plus two of the group	Plus three of the group
Producers		1	1	1	1	1	1	1	3	1	1	6	1	1	1	1	1	1	4	3
Musicians excluding band		2	1	2	1	6	2	22	27	68	71	40	6	24	45	52	46	2	48	27

wikipedia.org

BEATLES MONKEES BACKSTREET BOYS ONE DIRECTION

Year	1970	'70	'70	1980	'87	1990	'96	'96	'97	'97	'99	2000	'00	'05	'07	'09	'11	'12	'13	'13	Totals			
Album	Let It Be	Changes		Pool It!		Justus	Backstreet Boys	Backstreet's Back	Backstreet Boys (US)	Millennium		Black & Blue	Never Gone	Unbreakable	This is Us	Up All Night	Take Me Home	Midnight Memories	In A World Like This		12 LPs	11 LPs	9 LPs	3 LPs
	16	12		12		12	16	13	11	16		14	15	18	15	13	13	14	16		184	137	134	40
	0	8		14		0	27	15	17	18		16	28	26	34	27	29	-	23		33	112	134	66
notes		Plus one of the group		Plus two of the group																			Different ones	
	1	4		1		0	6	4	7	9		7	14	11	16	16	14	-	7		1	9	58	36
	52	22		9		0	2	-	-	24		-	-	-	-	1	-	-	-		274	301	26	1

105

DEGREES OF SEPARATION:
RIHANNA

She's the biggest R&B star ever to emerge from Barbados and conquered the world's music markets with an Umbrella. Little wonder perhaps, since she's only six degrees of separation from Princess Diana, Leonard Cohen, Indiana Jones, Alfred Hitchcock and Herman Melville.

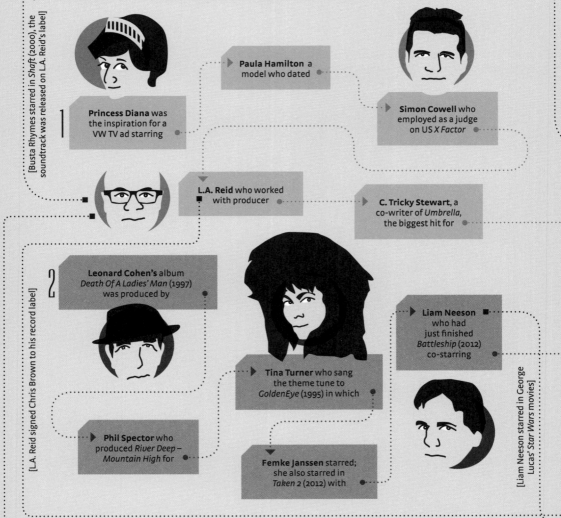

[Busta Rhymes starred in *Shaft* (2000), the soundtrack was released on L.A. Reid's label]

Paula Hamilton a model who dated

Simon Cowell who employed as a judge on US *X Factor*

1 **Princess Diana** was the inspiration for a VW TV ad starring

L.A. Reid who worked with producer

C. Tricky Stewart, a co-writer of *Umbrella*, the biggest hit for

[L.A. Reid signed Chris Brown to his record label]

2 **Leonard Cohen's** album *Death Of A Ladies' Man* (1997) was produced by

Liam Neeson who had just finished *Battleship* (2012) co-starring

Tina Turner who sang the theme tune to *GoldenEye* (1995) in which

[Liam Neeson starred in George Lucas' *Star Wars* movies]

Phil Spector who produced *River Deep – Mountain High* for

Femke Janssen starred; she also starred in *Taken 2* (2012) with

[Jay-Z was made head of Def Jam Recordings by L.A. Reid]

Janet Leigh
who is the mother of

5

Herman Melville's
Moby Dick was made
into a movie starring

4

Alfred Hitchcock
directed *Psycho* in
1960, which starred

John Houston,
who in
1982 directed
Annie starring

Jamie Lee Curtis
who starred in *Halloween:
Resurrection* (2002) with

Gregory Peck,
and directed by

Aileen Quinn,
who sang *Hard
Knock Life*, which
was sampled by

Busta Rhymes
who guested on the song
Look At Me Now by

[Evan Rogers introduced
Rihanna to Jay-Z]

Jay-Z for *Hard Knock Life
(Ghetto Anthem)*; he gave a
recording contract to

Chris Brown
one-time boyfriend of

Rihanna

Evan Rogers who is
credited with discovering

George Lucas
the director, who gave
an internship on *Raiders
Of The Lost Ark* (1984) to

Donny Osmond, the song
was co-produced by

Michael Bay
the director of the video
for *Soldier Of Love* by

3
Indiana Jones
was created by

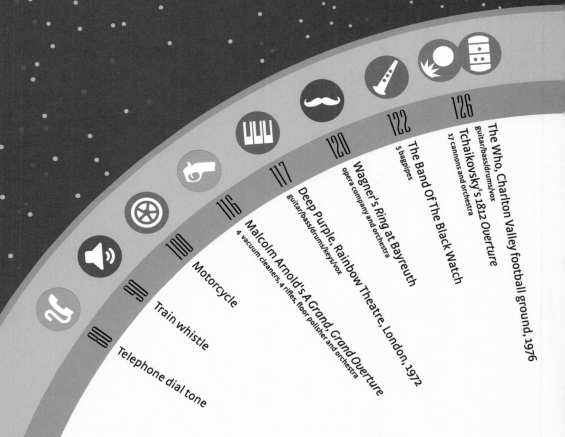

126

The Who, Charlton Valley football ground, 1976
guitar/bass/drums/vox

Tchaikovsky's 1812 Overture
17 cannons and orchestra

122

The Band Of The Black Watch
5 bagpipes

120

Wagner's Ring at Bayreuth
opera company and orchestra

117

Deep Purple, Rainbow Theatre, London, 1972
guitar/bass/drums/keys/vox

116

Malcolm Arnold's A Grand, Grand Overture
4 vacuum cleaners, 4 rifles, floor polisher and orchestra

100

Motorcycle

90

Train whistle

80

Telephone dial tone

LOUDER THAN **GOD**

It isn't only rock bands that leave audience's ears ringing. The classical world also has a few very, very loud performances, and made using some unusual instruments.

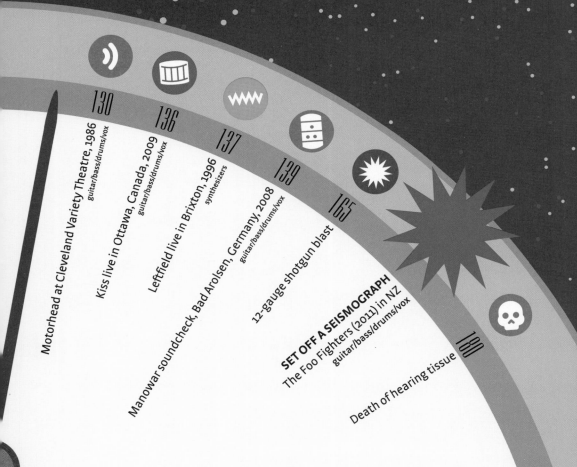

130 Motorhead at Cleveland Variety Theatre, 1986
guitar/bass/drums/vox

136 Kiss live in Ottawa, Canada, 2009
guitar/bass/drums/vox

137 Leftfield live in Brixton, 1996
synthesizers

139 Manowar soundcheck, Bad Arolsen, Germany, 2008
guitar/bass/drums/vox

165 12-gauge shotgun blast

SET OFF A SEISMOGRAPH
The Foo Fighters (2011) in NZ
guitar/bass/drums/vox

180 Death of hearing tissue

COMPARISON OF DECIBELS

sfu.ca, chem.purdue.edu, condor.admin.ccny.cuny.edu, wikipedia.org

CLASSICS GO **POP**

*Pop music of the late 20th century has found more than just
inspiration in classical music. In these instances it has taken whole
chunks of a composer's work and set it to a disco, rock and pop beat.*

YEAR	ORIGINAL TITLE / COMPOSER
c.1694	Canon In D Major / **Pachelbel**
c.1717	Orchestral Suite No.3, Air / **Bach**
c.1717	Prelude In F Minor (BWV 881) / **Bach**
1723	Jesu, Joy Of Man's Desiring / **Bach**
1725	Notebook For Anna Magdalena Bach / **Bach**
c.1780	Op. 36, 6 Sonatinas For Piano / **Clementi**
1784	Plaisir d'Amour / **Martini**
1801	Moonlight Sonata / **Beethoven**
1808	Fifth Symphony / **Beethoven**
1810	Für Elise / **Beethoven**
c.1826	Frühlingslied / **Mendelssohn**
1839	Prelude In C Minor (Prelude #20: Largo) / **Chopin**
1867	Night On Bald Mountain / **Mussorgsky**
1874	Pictures At An Exhibition / **Mussorgsky**
1892	March Of The Toy Soldiers / **Tchaikovsky**
1896	Also Sprach Zarathustra / **Strauss**
1898	O Sole Mio / **di Capua**
1901	Piano Concerto No.2 In C minor / **Rachmaninoff**
1927	Romance, Lieutenant Kijé / **Prokofiev**
1936	Adagio For Strings / **Barber**

ARTIST / TITLE	YEAR
Elvis Presley / It's Now Or Never	1960
Elvis Presley / Can't Help Falling In Love	1961
B. Bumble & The Stingers / Nut Rocker	1962
The Mindbenders / A Groovy Kind Of Love	1965
The Toys / A Lover's Concerto	1965
Procol Harum / A Whiter Shade Of Pale	1967
The Beatles / Because	1969
David Ruffin / My Whole World Ended	1969
Emerson, Lake & Palmer / Pictures At An Exhibition	1972
Deodato / Also Sprach Zarathustra	1972
Barry Manilow / Could It Be Magic	1975
Eric Carmen / All By Myself	1975
Walter Murphy / A Fifth Of Beethoven	1976
David Shire / Night On Disco Mountain	1976
Village People / Go West	1979
The Beach Boys / Lady Lynda	1979
Sting / Russians	1985
Oasis / Don't Look Back In Anger	1996
Coolio / C U When U Get There	1997
William Orbit / Barber's Adagio For Strings	1999
Nas / I Can	2003
Jem / They	2005

SAMPLE **THIS**

MOST SAMPLED SONGS

Rank/Samples/Original date of release/Artist name/Song name

Rank		Samples	Year	Artist	Song
1		184	1970	James Brown	Funky Drummer
2		127	1968	Sly & The Family Stone	
3		116	1972	The Honey Drippers	Impeach The President
4		112	1972	Lyn Collins	
5		100	1974	James Brown	Funky President (People It's Bad)
6		94	1973	Melvin Bliss	
7		80	1982	George Clinton	Atomic Dog
8		74	1971	Kool & The Gang	
9		71	1972	The Emotions	Blind Alley
10		67	1974	James Brown	
11		63	1976	Bob James	Nautilus
12		60	1973	Skull Snaps	
13		59	1981	ESG	UFO
14		59	1978	Parliament	
15		59	1970	James Brown	Get Up, Get Into It, Get Involved
16		51	1980	Zapp	
17		50	1972	Bobby Byrd	I'm Coming, I'm Coming, I'm Coming
18		50	1973	The Ohio Players	
19		46	1968	The Mohawks	The Champ
20		46	1973	The Incredible Bongo Band	Apache

Sing A Simple Song
Think (About It)
Synthetic Substitution
N.T.
The Payback
It's A New Day
Flash Light
More Bounce To The Ounce
Funky Worm

DJs, mixers and artists who use **the-breaks.com** listed 15,083 different samples by 3,036 artists from 3,847 albums. The most sampled turned out to be predominantly from the first era of funk, the late 1960s and 1970s.

MOST SAMPLED ARTISTS
Rank/Samples/Artist name

Kool & The Gang
Sly & The Family Stone
Bob James
Isaac Hayes
The Ohio Players
The Honey Drippers
Lou Donaldson
Curtis Mayfield
The Isley Brothers
Quincy Jones

James Brown

Washington Grover Jr.
Roy Ayers (Ubiquity)
Zapp
The Average White Band
The Meters
Lyn Collins
Funkadelic
The J.B.'s
Parliament

907
280
198
184
147
133
116
110
101
97

294
254
195
183
136
116
113
104
101
97

1
3
5
7
9
11
13
15
17
19

2
4
6
8
10
12
14
16
18
20

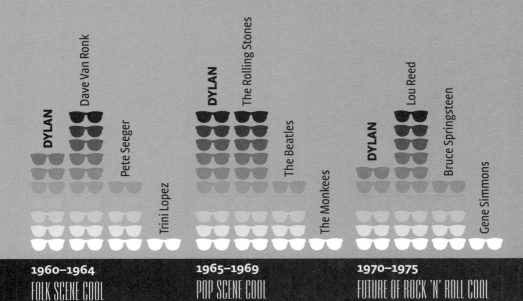

DYLAN · Dave Van Ronk · Pete Seeger · Trini Lopez

1960–1964
FOLK SCENE COOL

DYLAN · The Rolling Stones · The Beatles · The Monkees

1965–1969
POP SCENE COOL

DYLAN · Lou Reed · Bruce Springsteen · Gene Simmons

1970–1975
FUTURE OF ROCK 'N' ROLL COOL

THE COOL OF **DYLAN**

Bob Dylan is arguably the longest-touring rock 'n' roll icon left – he even predates The Rolling Stones. Throughout his long and varied career he has been considered very cool, but not always. A panel of eminent rock critics have voted on Dylan's cool quotient at significant periods of his career.

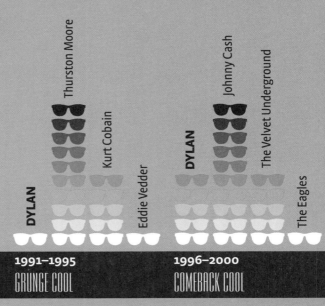

Thurston Moore · Kurt Cobain · Eddie Vedder · **DYLAN**

1991–1995
GRUNGE COOL

DYLAN · Johnny Cash · The Velvet Underground · The Eagles

1996–2000
COMEBACK COOL

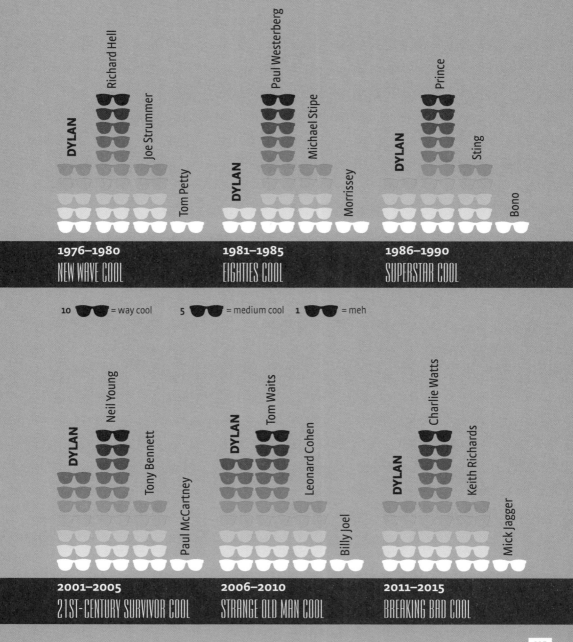

Richard Hell

DYLAN

Joe Strummer

Tom Petty

1976–1980
NEW WAVE COOL

Paul Westerberg

DYLAN

Michael Stipe

Morrissey

1981–1985
EIGHTIES COOL

Prince

DYLAN

Sting

Bono

1986–1990
SUPERSTAR COOL

10 = way cool   5 = medium cool   1 = meh

Neil Young

DYLAN

Tony Bennett

Paul McCartney

2001–2005
21ST-CENTURY SURVIVOR COOL

Tom Waits

DYLAN

Leonard Cohen

Billy Joel

2006–2010
STRANGE OLD MAN COOL

Charlie Watts

DYLAN

Keith Richards

Mick Jagger

2011–2015
BREAKING BAD COOL

115

CLASSICAL CENTENARY
CELEBRATIONS

The best way to make a marketing splash with classical music is to promote a centenary event, preferably for the whole year. These classical composers and their birth places will be able to celebrate the centenary of their birth, death, or both, in the coming century.

♩ Centenary Celebration

♫ Double Centenary Celebration

♫ Triple Centenary Celebration

♫ Quadruple Centenary Celebration

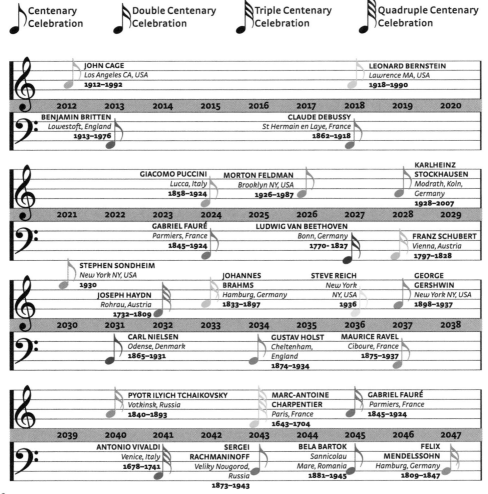

JOHN CAGE
Los Angeles CA, USA
1912–1992

LEONARD BERNSTEIN
Lawrence MA, USA
1918–1990

2012	2013	2014	2015	2016	2017	2018	2019	2020

BENJAMIN BRITTEN
Lowestoft, England
1913–1976

CLAUDE DEBUSSY
St Hermain en Laye, France
1862–1918

KARLHEINZ STOCKHAUSEN
Modrath, Koln, Germany
1928–2007

GIACOMO PUCCINI
Lucca, Italy
1858–1924

MORTON FELDMAN
Brooklyn NY, USA
1926–1987

2021	2022	2023	2024	2025	2026	2027	2028	2029

GABRIEL FAURÉ
Parmiers, France
1845–1924

LUDWIG VAN BEETHOVEN
Bonn, Germany
1770- 1827

FRANZ SCHUBERT
Vienna, Austria
1797–1828

STEPHEN SONDHEIM
New York NY, USA
1930

JOHANNES BRAHMS
Hamburg, Germany
1833–1897

STEVE REICH
New York NY, USA
1936

GEORGE GERSHWIN
New York NY, USA
1898–1937

JOSEPH HAYDN
Rohrau, Austria
1732–1809

2030	2031	2032	2033	2034	2035	2036	2037	2038

CARL NIELSEN
Odense, Denmark
1865–1931

GUSTAV HOLST
Cheltenham, England
1874–1934

MAURICE RAVEL
Ciboure, France
1875–1937

PYOTR ILYICH TCHAIKOVSKY
Votkinsk, Russia
1840–1893

MARC-ANTOINE CHARPENTIER
Paris, France
1643–1704

GABRIEL FAURÉ
Parmiers, France
1845–1924

2039	2040	2041	2042	2043	2044	2045	2046	2047

ANTONIO VIVALDI
Venice, Italy
1678–1741

SERGEI RACHMANINOFF
Veliky Nougorod, Russia
1873–1943

BELA BARTOK
Sannicolau Mare, Romania
1881–1945

FELIX MENDELSSOHN
Hamburg, Germany
1809–1847

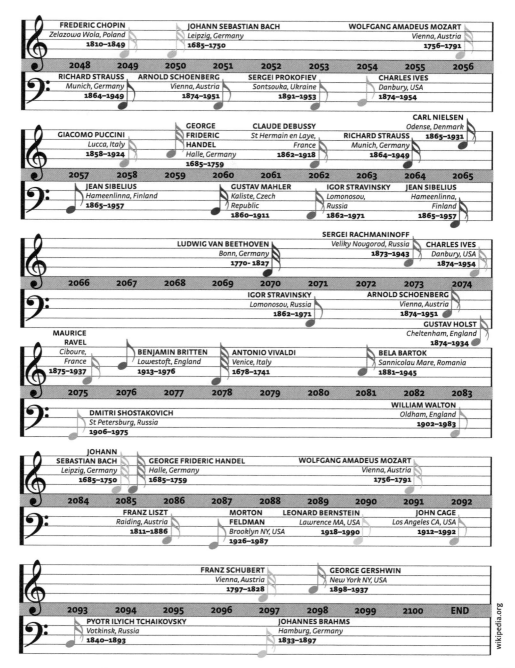

FREDERIC CHOPIN
Zelazowa Wola, Poland
1810–1849

JOHANN SEBASTIAN BACH
Leipzig, Germany
1685–1750

WOLFGANG AMADEUS MOZART
Vienna, Austria
1756–1791

2048 2049 2050 2051 2052 2053 2054 2055 2056

RICHARD STRAUSS
Munich, Germany
1864–1949

ARNOLD SCHOENBERG
Vienna, Austria
1874–1951

SERGEI PROKOFIEV
Sontsovka, Ukraine
1891–1953

CHARLES IVES
Danbury, USA
1874–1954

GIACOMO PUCCINI
Lucca, Italy
1858–1924

GEORGE
FRIDERIC
HANDEL
Halle, Germany
1685–1759

CLAUDE DEBUSSY
St Hermain en Laye,
France
1862–1918

RICHARD STRAUSS
Munich, Germany
1864–1949

CARL NIELSEN
Odense, Denmark
1865–1931

2057 2058 2059 2060 2061 2062 2063 2064 2065

JEAN SIBELIUS
Hameenlinna, Finland
1865–1957

GUSTAV MAHLER
Kaliste, Czech
Republic
1860–1911

IGOR STRAVINSKY
Lomonosou,
Russia
1862–1971

JEAN SIBELIUS
Hameenlinna,
Finland
1865–1957

LUDWIG VAN BEETHOVEN
Bonn, Germany
1770- 1827

SERGEI RACHMANINOFF
Veliky Nougorod, Russia
1873–1943

CHARLES IVES
Danbury, USA
1874–1954

2066 2067 2068 2069 2070 2071 2072 2073 2074

IGOR STRAVINSKY
Lomonosou, Russia
1862–1971

ARNOLD SCHOENBERG
Vienna, Austria
1874–1951

MAURICE
RAVEL
Ciboure,
France
1875–1937

BENJAMIN BRITTEN
Lowestoft, England
1913–1976

ANTONIO VIVALDI
Venice, Italy
1678–1741

GUSTAV HOLST
Cheltenham, England
1874–1934

BELA BARTOK
Sannicolau Mare, Romania
1881–1945

2075 2076 2077 2078 2079 2080 2081 2082 2083

DMITRI SHOSTAKOVICH
St Petersburg, Russia
1906–1975

WILLIAM WALTON
Oldham, England
1902–1983

JOHANN
SEBASTIAN BACH
Leipzig, Germany
1685–1750

GEORGE FRIDERIC HANDEL
Halle, Germany
1685–1759

WOLFGANG AMADEUS MOZART
Vienna, Austria
1756–1791

2084 2085 2086 2087 2088 2089 2090 2091 2092

FRANZ LISZT
Raiding, Austria
1811–1886

MORTON
FELDMAN
Brooklyn NY, USA
1926–1987

LEONARD BERNSTEIN
Lawrence MA, USA
1918–1990

JOHN CAGE
Los Angeles CA, USA
1912–1992

FRANZ SCHUBERT
Vienna, Austria
1797–1828

GEORGE GERSHWIN
New York NY, USA
1898–1937

2093 2094 2095 2096 2097 2098 2099 2100 END

PYOTR ILYICH TCHAIKOVSKY
Votkinsk, Russia
1840–1893

JOHANNES BRAHMS
Hamburg, Germany
1833–1897

DAVID BOWIE **IS**

The former David Jones of Brixton became famous as Ziggy Stardust from Mars and then so many other persona during a remarkably long and varied career.

1976

'Station To Station'
The Thin White Duke

1975

'Young Americans'
'The Man Who Fell To Earth'

1973

'Aladdin Sane'
Ziggy retires

1974   'Diamond Dogs'

1972

'The Rise And Fall Of Ziggy Stardust And The Spiders From Mars'

'David Bowie'
(Mercury Records).
'Space Oddity'
Marries Angie

1971   **1970**

'Hunky Dory'
'Life on Mars'

'The Man Who Sold The World'
Banned sleeve

1969

START

1947

David Jones, born in Brixton (London)

1958

Attends Bromley Technical High School

1963-67

First bands:
The Konrads, Davie Jones and the King Bees, The Manish Boys, Davy Jones and the Lower Third, David Bowie and the Buzz, The Riot Squad

1967

First album:
'David Bowie'
(Deram)

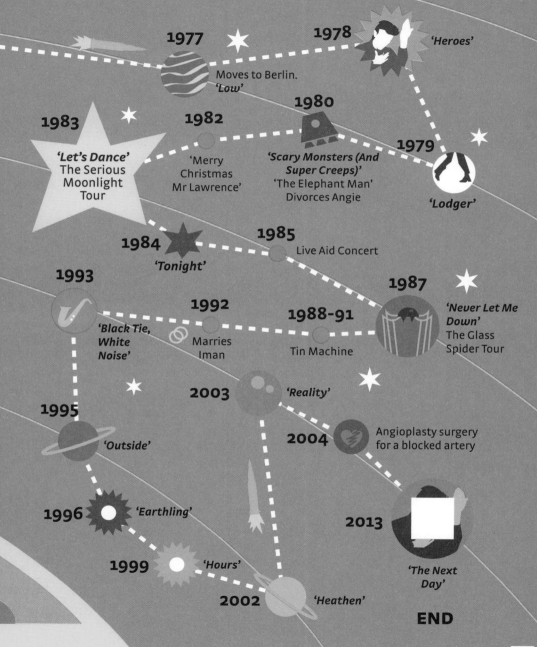

1977
Moves to Berlin.
'Low'

1978
'Heroes'

1980
'Scary Monsters (And Super Creeps)'
'The Elephant Man'
Divorces Angie

1979
'Lodger'

1983
'Let's Dance'
The Serious Moonlight Tour

1982
'Merry Christmas Mr Lawrence'

1984
'Tonight'

1985
Live Aid Concert

1993
'Black Tie, White Noise'

1992
Marries Iman

1988-91
Tin Machine

1987
'Never Let Me Down'
The Glass Spider Tour

1995
'Outside'

2003
'Reality'

2004
Angioplasty surgery for a blocked artery

1996
'Earthling'

1999
'Hours'

2013
'The Next Day'

2002
'Heathen'

END

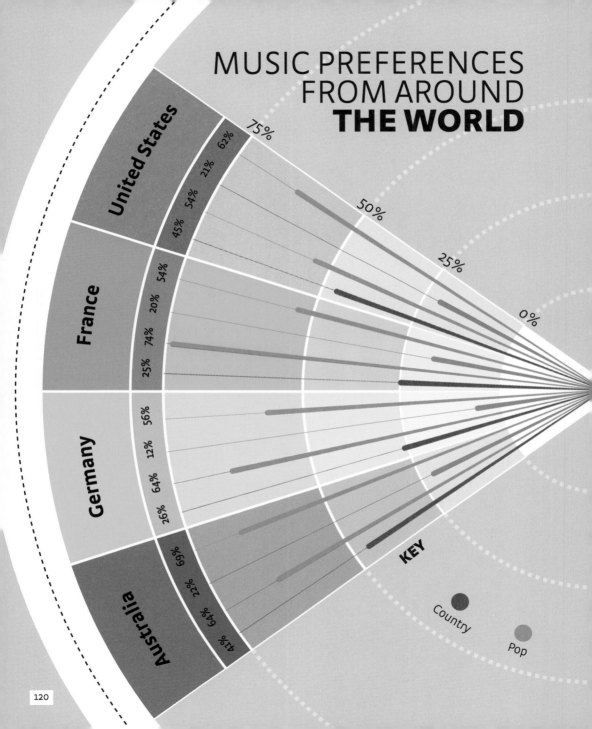

MUSIC PREFERENCES FROM AROUND **THE WORLD**

75%

50%

25%

0%

United States
62%
21%
54%
45%

France
54%
20%
74%
25%

Germany
56%
12%
64%
26%

Australia
69%
22%
64%
41%

KEY

Country

Pop

120

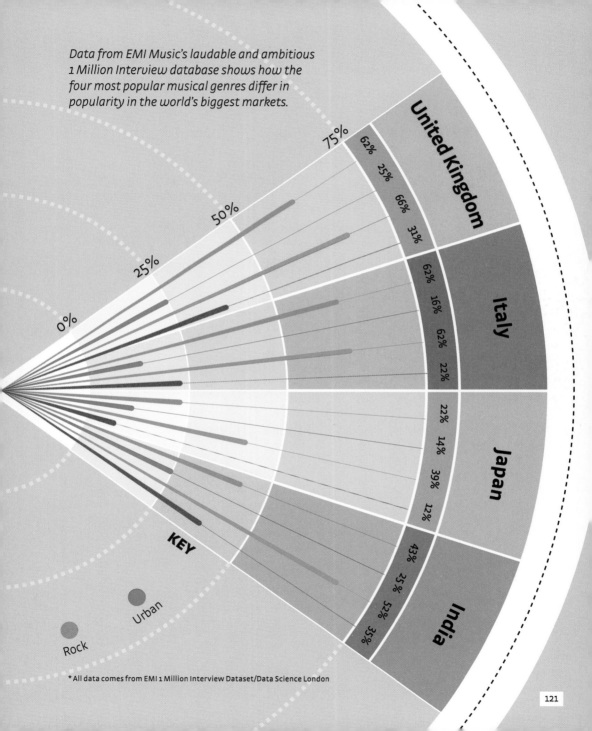

Data from EMI Music's laudable and ambitious 1 Million Interview database shows how the four most popular musical genres differ in popularity in the world's biggest markets.

75%

50%

25%

0%

United Kingdom
62%
25%
66%
31%

Italy
62%
16%
62%
22%

Japan
22%
14%
39%
12%

India
43%
25%
52%
35%

KEY

Urban

Rock

* All data comes from EMI 1 Million Interview Dataset/Data Science London

IT TAKES **TWO**

To make a music superstar, just ask Elvis, Bob or One Direction. Here are the music business' most successful managers and the artists they've helped become successful.

THE ROLLING STONES - $140 MILLION — ALLEN KLEIN

Born in New Jersey (1941–2009) the son of a butcher, he trained as an accountant and helped Sam Cooke form his own record company, and subsequently became one of the first business managers in music. He took over The Rolling Stones' business affairs after promising to find millions of dollars owing to them by auditing all of their accounts. He did the same for The Beatles and oversaw the break-up of the band. He served two months in prison in 1979 for tax evasion.

LED ZEPPELIN - $400 MILLION — PETER GRANT

A huge bear of a man, Grant (1935–1995) used his size to intimidate his bands' promoters and record companies. He learned about artist management from Don Arden (father of Sharon Osbourne) who favoured hanging reluctant debtors from upstairs windows by their ankles until they paid him. Made Led Zep the biggest band in the world and demanded 90% of all money from live gigs for them. Colonel Parker asked him to organize a European tour for Elvis, but the King died before it could happen.

ELVIS PRESLEY - $4.5 BILLION — COL TOM PARKER

Real name Andreas Cornelis van Kuijk (1909–1997), an illegal immigrant and carnival barker, he was one of the first rock'n'roll managers. Began his career managing country singers Gene Austin and Hank Snow before spotting the potential in Elvis.

ONE DIRECTION - $1 BILLION — MODEST MGMT

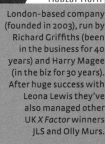

London-based company (founded in 2003), run by Richard Griffiths (been in the business for 40 years) and Harry Magee (in the biz for 30 years). After huge success with Leona Lewis they've also managed other UK *X Factor* winners JLS and Olly Murs.

DAVID BOWIE - $215 MILLION — TONY DEFRIES

British-born (c.1945) music entrepreneur who learned the business in the mid-1960s, helped turn Bowie into Ziggy and aided the careers of, among others, Iggy Pop, Lou Reed, Mott The Hoople and The New Seekers. Since 2008 he has run a company developing solar-power technology.

BACKSTREET BOYS - $200 MILLION — LOU PEARLMAN

American Pearlman (b.1954) is currently serving 25 years in prison for operating one of America's biggest and longest-running Ponzi schemes (worth $300m). Prior to that he helped make Backstreet Boys and N'Sync hugely successful pop stars.

THE BEATLES - $2.2 BILLION — BRIAN EPSTEIN

Liverpool-born Epstein (1934–1967), the son of furniture dealers, helped to run a store selling musical instruments and washing machines until spotting the leather-clad Beatles in the Cavern. He made them dress nicely and got them signed to EMI. He once offered the band a wage of £50 for life. Epstein died of an accidental barbiturate overdose.

THE SPICE GIRLS - $21 MILLION — SIMON FULLER

Perhaps best known as the creator of the 'Idol' TV show format, British born Fuller (1960–) signed Madonna to her UK record label in 1983 and in 1985 formed the management company '19'. He didn't discover The Spice Girls, but he made them successful. He's also managed Annie Lennox and the Beckhams.

THE SEX PISTOLS - $5 MILLION — MALCOLM MCLAREN

British-born McLaren (1946–2010), the son of a rag-trade merchant, was an art school dropout and clothes store owner who liked to spread the idea that he invented punk rock. He didn't, but he did get The Sex Pistols into tabloid newspapers.

BOB DYLAN - $180 MILLION — ALBERT GROSSMAN

Chicagoan Grossman (1926–1986) turned America's folk music scene into a world-beating phenomenon and launched the careers of Bob Dylan, The Band, Peter, Paul & Mary and Janis Joplin. He died of a heart attack, while flying on Concorde.

wikipedia.org

THE BIG **VINYL**
FIGHTBACK

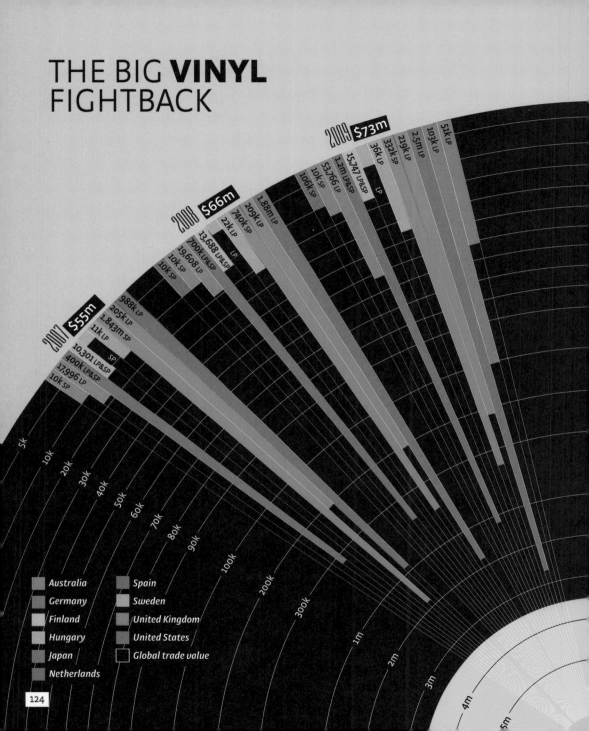

2007 $55m

- 988k LP
- 205k SP
- 1.843m LP
- 11k LP
- SP
- 10,301 LP&SP
- 400k LP&SP
- 17,996 LP
- 10k SP

2008 $66m

- 10k SP
- 19,608 LP
- 700k LP&SP
- 13,688 LP&SP
- LP
- 22k LP
- 740k SP
- 209k LP
- 1.188m LP

2009 $73m

- 106k SP
- 10k SP
- 53,766 LP
- 1.2m LP&SP
- 15,747 LP&SP
- 36k LP
- LP
- 332k SP
- 2.5m LP
- 219k LP
- 103k LP
- 51k LP

5k
10k
20k
30k
40k
50k
60k
70k
80k
90k
100k
200k
300k
1m
2m
3m
4m
5m

Legend:
- Australia
- Germany
- Finland
- Hungary
- Japan
- Netherlands
- Spain
- Sweden
- United Kingdom
- United States
- Global trade value

124

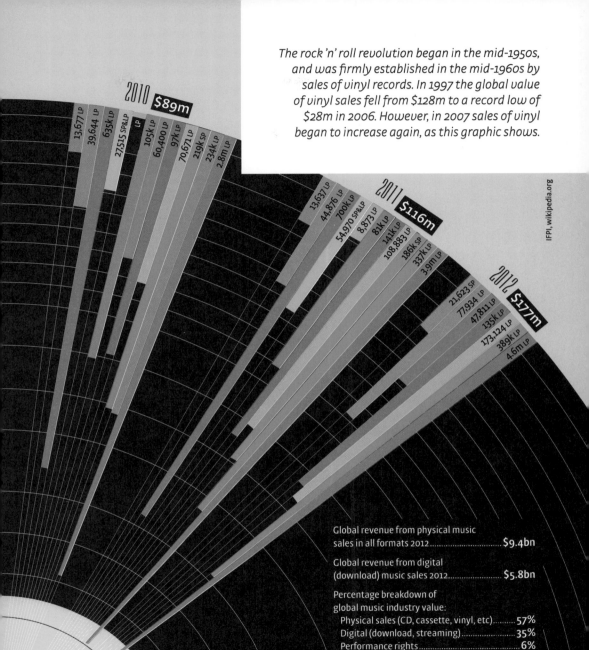

The rock 'n' roll revolution began in the mid-1950s, and was firmly established in the mid-1960s by sales of vinyl records. In 1997 the global value of vinyl sales fell from $128m to a record low of $28m in 2006. However, in 2007 sales of vinyl began to increase again, as this graphic shows.

IFPI, wikipedia.org

2010 $89m

13,677 LP
39,644 LP
635k LP
27,515 SP&LP
LP
105k LP
60,400 LP
97k LP
70,671 LP
219k SP
234k LP
2.8m LP

2011 $116m

13,637 LP
44,876 LP
700k LP
54,970 SP&LP
8,873 LP
81k LP
141k LP
108,883 LP
186k SP
337k LP
3.9m LP

2012 $177m

21,623 SP
77,934 LP
47,811 LP
135k LP
173,124 LP
389k LP
4.6m LP

Global revenue from physical music sales in all formats 2012 .... **$9.4bn**

Global revenue from digital (download) music sales 2012 .... **$5.8bn**

Percentage breakdown of global music industry value:
Physical sales (CD, cassette, vinyl, etc).......... **57%**
Digital (download, streaming) **35%**
Performance rights.. **6%**
Sync rights (advertising, etc)............................ **2%**

ROYALTY **CAKE**

Slicing up the royalties paid from the sale of a CD produces one cake.

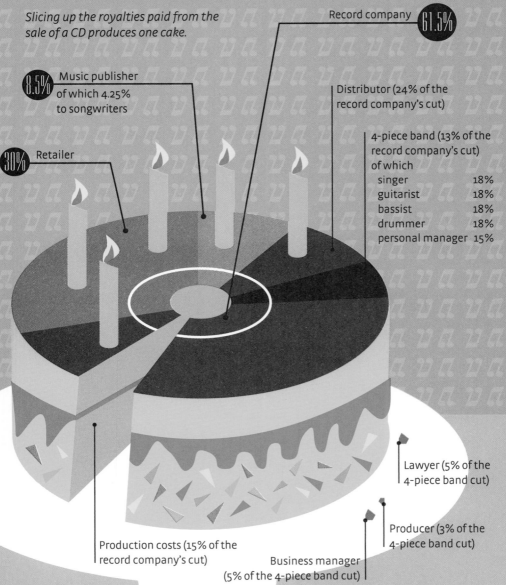

Record company **61.5%**

8.5% Music publisher
of which 4.25%
to songwriters

Distributor (24% of the
record company's cut)

30% Retailer

4-piece band (13% of the
record company's cut)
of which
  singer   18%
  guitarist   18%
  bassist   18%
  drummer   18%
  personal manager 15%

Lawyer (5% of the
4-piece band cut)

Producer (3% of the
4-piece band cut)

Production costs (15% of the
record company's cut)

Business manager
(5% of the 4-piece band cut)

COVER ME

Sometimes a song just doesn't work for its original performer, but someone else makes it a success. Everywhere. Here are six of the most successful cover versions of the past 40 years.

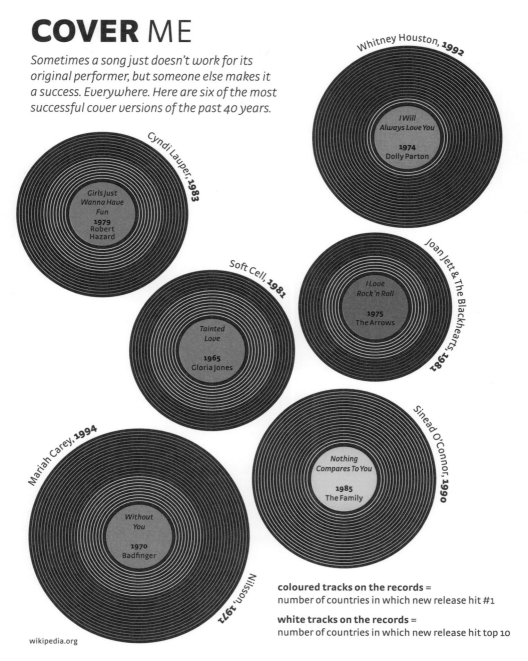

Whitney Houston, **1992**

I Will
Always Love You

1974
Dolly Parton

Cyndi Lauper, **1983**

Girls Just
Wanna Have
Fun

1979
Robert
Hazard

Soft Cell, **1981**

Tainted
Love

1965
Gloria Jones

Joan Jett & The Blackhearts, **1981**

I Love
Rock 'n Roll

1975
The Arrows

Sinead O'Connor, **1990**

Nothing
Compares To You

1985
The Family

Mariah Carey, **1994**

Without
You

1970
Badfinger

Nilsson, **1971**

coloured tracks on the records =
number of countries in which new release hit #1

white tracks on the records =
number of countries in which new release hit top 10

wikipedia.org

ACTS WHO MANAGED TO PLACE ONLY ONCE IN THE TOP 10

HIGHEST POSITION	#	Act *Only Top 10 single* (year)	☆ = 10th in the charts ☆☆☆☆☆☆☆☆☆☆ = 1st in the charts
	9	**The Who** *I Can See For Miles* (**1967**)	
	4	**Led Zeppelin** *Whole Lotta Love* (**1970**)	
	1	**Janis Joplin** *Me and Bobby McGee* (**1971**)	
	1	**Neil Young** *Heart Of Gold* (**1972**)	
	7	**Joni Mitchell** *Help Me* (**1975**)	
	8	**Lynyrd Skynyrd** *Sweet Home Alabama* (**1974**)	
	3	**Boz Scaggs** *Lowdown* (**1976**)	
	1	**Pink Floyd** *Another Brick In The Wall* (**1980**)	
	5	**Willie Nelson** *Always On My Mind* (**1982**)	
	8	**The Clash** *Rock The Casbah* (**1983**)	
	9	**Grateful Dead** *Touch Of Grey* (**1987**)	
	2	**The Cure** *Love Song* (**1989**)	
	7	**Tom Petty** *Free Fallin'* (**1989**)	
	6	**Nirvana** *Smells Like Teen Spirit* (**1991**)	
	10	**Metallica** *Until It Sleeps* (**1996**)	
	5	**Garth Brooks** *Lost In You* (**1999**)	
	2	**Daft Punk** *Get Lucky* (**2013**)	

wikipedia.org

ONE AND NONE
HIT WONDERS

The biggest singles market in the world has always been American and the most important chart the Billboard Hot 100. The list of acts who managed to place on it only once or not at all is long – and surprising.

ACTS WHO NEVER MANAGED TO PLACE IN THE TOP 10

HIGHEST POSITION	#	Act / Ranking in the Top 100 (year)	☆ = 51st in the charts ☆ x 50 = 1st in the charts
	15	**B.B. King** / *The Thrill Is Gone* **(1970)**	
	20	**Jimi Hendrix** / *All Along The Watchtower* **(1968)**	
	51	**Bob Marley** / *Roots Rock Reggae* **(1976)**	
	18	**Nina Simone** / *I Loves You, Porgy* **(1959)**	
	23	**AC/DC** / *Moneytalks* **(1990)**	
	30	**Kate Bush** / *Running Up That Hill* **(1985)**	
	19	**Elvis Costello** / *Veronica* **(1989)**	
	28	**Iggy Pop** / *Candy* **(1990)**	
	46	**Morrissey** / *The More You Ignore Me* **(1992)**	
	34	**Radiohead** / *Creep* **(1992)**	

ACTS THAT NEVER CHARTED

The Velvet Underground   The Sex Pistols   Motorhead   New York Dolls   Tom Waits

RINGO STARR – THE BEATLES

HEIGHT 1.68m/5ft 6in

Ludwig four-piece kit

DRUM	DEPTH	WIDTH
KICK DRUM	35.6cm/14in	50.8cm/20in
SNARE	14cm/5 1/2in	35.6cm/14in
RACK TOM	20.3cm/8in	30.5cm/12in
FLOOR TOM	35.6cm/14in	35.6cm/14in

CHARLIE WATTS – THE ROLLING STONES

HEIGHT 1.73m/5ft 8in

Gretsch four-piece kit

DRUM	DEPTH	WIDTH
KICK DRUM	35.6cm/14in	55.9cm/22in
SNARE	12.7cm/5in	35.6cm/14in
RACK TOM	20.3cm/8in	30.5cm/12in
FLOOR TOM	35.6cm/14in	40.6cm/16in

JOHN BONHAM – LED ZEPPELIN

HEIGHT 1.79m/5ft 10in

Ludwig five-piece kit

DRUM	DEPTH	WIDTH
KICK DRUM	35.6cm/14in	66cm/26in
SNARE	16.5cm/6 1/2in	35.6cm/14in
RACK TOM	30.5cm/12in	35.6cm/14in
FLOOR TOM	40.6cm/16in	40.6cm/16in
FLOOR TOM	40.6cm/16in	45.7cm/18in

DOES SIZE **MATTER?**

Comparing the four best-known rock drummers that the business has ever known via their height and the tools of their trade, it appears that height equates to kit size until you get to Keith Moon, who over-reached himself in all directions.

KEITH MOON – THE WHO

HEIGHT 1.76m/5ft 6in

Premier Custom nine-piece kit

DRUM	DEPTH	WIDTH
KICK DRUM	35.6cm/14in	55.9cm/22in
KICK DRUM	35.6cm/14in	55.9cm/22in
SNARE	14cm/5½in	35.6cm/14in
RACK TOM	20.3cm/8in	35.6cm/14in
RACK TOM	20.3cm/8in	35.6cm/14in
RACK TOM	20.3cm/8in	35.6cm/14in
FLOOR TOM	40.6cm/16in	40.6cm/16in
FLOOR TOM	40.6cm/16in	45.7cm/18in
FLOOR TOM	40.6cm/16in	45.7cm/18in

thewho.net, johnbonham.co.uk, gretschdrums.com, ringosbeatleskits.com

1952
Konkrete Etude
Karlheinz Stockhausen,
Switzerland
*first recording
to use cut-and-splice
tape technique
with electronically
generated sounds*

1953
Nordwestdeutscher
Rundfunk studio
(RDFW)
Cologne, Germany
*equipped with electronic
sound generators and
modifiers, centre of
German electronic music*

1956
Forbidden Planet
Original Soundtrack
Louis and Bebe Barron,
US
*first purely electronic
film score*

1957
MUSIC-N
Max Mathews,
Bell Labs, US
*first computer program
for generating digital
audio waveforms
through direct synthesis*

1958
Electro-Theremin
Bob Whitsell, US
*adaptation of Theremin
using mechanical
not spatial input*

1959
Columbia-Princeton
Studio, New York
Vladimir Ussachevsky,
Russia
*Integrated RCA II,
the first voltage-
controlled
synthesizer*

1963
Dr Who Theme
Delia Derbyshire, BBC
Radiophonic Workshop,
UK
*electronic version of theme
tune by Ron Grainer*

Mellotron
Harry Chamberlin, US,
Frank, Norman and
Les Bradley, UK
*electro-mechanical
polyphonic tape
replay keyboard*

1964
Moog Synthesizer
Robert Moog, US
*first modular voltage-
controlled subtractive
synthesizer*

1967
Strawberry
Fields Forever
The Beatles, UK
use of Mellotron

Nights In White Satin
The Moody Blues, UK
use of Mellotron

Pet Sounds
The Beach Boys, US
*extensive use of
Electro-Theremin*

1968
Switched On Bach
Wendy Carlos, US
*first classical recording
made using synthesizers;
first classical record to
sell over 500,000 copies*

1969
Moog 950B Scale
Programmer
Robert Moog, US
*real-time device for
stabilizing the notes
within a range during
a performance*

1971
ARP 2600
Alan R. Pearlman,
Dennis Colin, US
*semi-modular subtractive
synthesizer marketed
at beginners*

1973
Synclavier
New England Digital
Corp., US
*prototype digital
synthesizer
and polyphonic digital
sampling system*

1974
Autobahn
Kratfwerk, Germany
*internationally
successful album and
hit single, extensive
use of Minimoog
and similar synths,
originator of Krautrock*

Phaedra
Tangerine Dream,
Germany
*internationally successful
album, extensive use of
Mellotron and Moog,
originator of synth-rock*

1975
Love To Love You Baby
Donna Summer, US,
Giorgio Moroder, Italy
*international hit, first
disco success to only use
all synthesized
instruments*

1976
Oxygéne
Jean Michel Jarre, France
*ARP 2600-driven proto
ambient international hit*

1978
Oberheim OB-1
Tom Oberheim, US
*first programmable
analog synth*

You Make Me Feel
(Mighty Real)
Sylvester, US
*international Hi-NRG
hit, all synthesized
with BPM 13-140*

1979
Fairlight CMI
Peter Vogel, Kim Ryrie,
Tony Furse, Australia
first sampler workstation

Cars
Gary Numan, UK
*international new-
wave hit, Minimoog
and Polymoog*

Solid State Survivor
Yellow Magic Orchestra,
Japan
*Roland TR-808 drum-
driven hit, beginning
the electro genre*

A HISTORY OF
ELECTRONIC
MUSIC

Synthesizers, drum machines, sequencers and Auto-Tune are today all commonly used in making music, and without them many a star might be nothing more than burger-flipping dreamers. Here's how electricity was harnessed in the making of music and the key releases of electronic music genres.

1980
Linn LM-1
Roger Linn, US
first drum machine to use digital samples of real drums

Roland TR808
Roland Corporation, Japan
first cheap commercially available digital programmable drum machine

Vienna
Ultravox, UK
internationally successful album and single, recorded at Kraftwerk's studio in Cologne

1982
Prophet 600
Sequential Circuits, US
first MIDI synth

I Ran (So Far Away)
A Flock Of Seagulls, UK
first British synth-pop band to have a hit in the US

Roland TB-303
Roland Corp., Japan
bass synth with built-in sequencer

Planet Rock
Afrika Bambaataa, US
first hit rap single driven by TR-808, using Fairlight, Moog and Prophet synths

1983
Rip It Up
Orange Juice, UK
first hit single to use the TB-303

Six-Trak
Sequential Circuits, US
first multi-timbral synth with MIDI and sequencers

Yamaha DX7
Yamaha Corporation, Japan
first popular cheap digital synth

1985
Atari ST
Atari Corp, US
first home computer with integrated MIDI support

1985
Take On Me
A-Ha, Norway
Fairlight-driven synth-pop international hit

1987
Acid Tracks
Phuture, US
use of TB-303, crested Acid House sound

1989
Proteus 1
E-Mu Systems, US
first commercially available Read Only Memory (ROM) sampler

Waldorf Microwave
Waldorf Music, Germany
first commercial wavetable synth

Sound Tools
Evan Brooks, Peter Gotcher, Digi Design, US
computer-based stereo audio editor software for the Apple Mac launched

1991
Pro Tools
Digi Design, US
multitrack update of Sound Tools launched

1997
Auto-Tune
Andy Hildebrand, Antares Audio Technologies, US
audio processor measuring and correcting pitch for vocals and instruments

1998
Believe
Cher, US
first commercial release to use Auto-Tune

Moon Safari
Air, France
inspired retro-electronica acts using 1980s-era synths

synthmuseum.com, acousmata.com, historyofrecording.com, richardhess.com, mixonline.com, newworldrecords.org, wikipedia.org

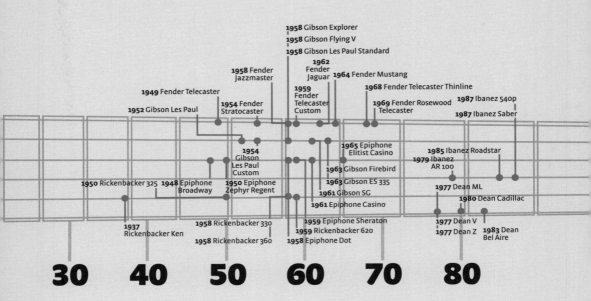

1958 Gibson Explorer
1958 Gibson Flying V
1958 Gibson Les Paul Standard

1958 Fender Jazzmaster
1962 Fender Jaguar
1964 Fender Mustang

1949 Fender Telecaster
1954 Fender Stratocaster
1959 Fender Telecaster Custom
1968 Fender Telecaster Thinline
1987 Ibanez 540p

1952 Gibson Les Paul
1969 Fender Rosewood Telecaster
1987 Ibanez Saber

1954 Gibson Les Paul Custom
1965 Epiphone Elitist Casino
1985 Ibanez Roadstar
1979 Ibanez AR 100

1950 Rickenbacker 325
1948 Epiphone Broadway
1950 Epiphone Zephyr Regent
1963 Gibson Firebird
1963 Gibson ES 335
1961 Gibson SG
1961 Epiphone Casino
1977 Dean ML
1980 Dean Cadillac

1937 Rickenbacker Ken
1958 Rickenbacker 330
1958 Rickenbacker 360
1959 Epiphone Sheraton
1959 Rickenbacker 620
1958 Epiphone Dot
1977 Dean V
1977 Dean Z
1983 Dean Bel Aire

30   40   50   60   70   80

FENDER   GIBSON   EPIPHONE

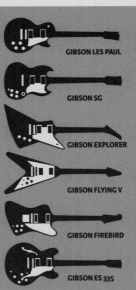

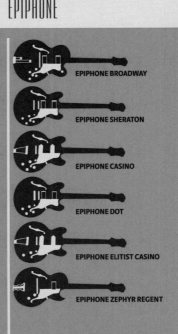

FENDER TELECASTER   GIBSON LES PAUL   EPIPHONE BROADWAY

FENDER STRATOCASTER   GIBSON SG   EPIPHONE SHERATON

FENDER JAGUAR   GIBSON EXPLORER   EPIPHONE CASINO

FENDER JAZZMASTER   GIBSON FLYING V   EPIPHONE DOT

FENDER MUSTANG   GIBSON FIREBIRD   EPIPHONE ELITIST CASINO

                        GIBSON ES 335   EPIPHONE ZEPHYR REGENT

ROCK OF **AGES**

More than any other instrument, the electric guitar has defined not just the sound, but also the look and cool quotient of popular music. Here's the six major guitar makers' key models produced since the 1930s.

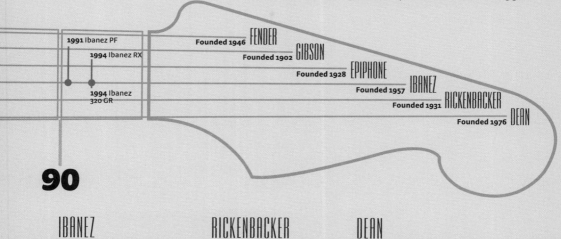

1991 Ibanez PF

1994 Ibanez RX

1994 Ibanez 320 GR

Founded 1946 FENDER

Founded 1902 GIBSON

Founded 1928 EPIPHONE

Founded 1957 IBANEZ

Founded 1931 RICKENBACKER

Founded 1976 DEAN

90

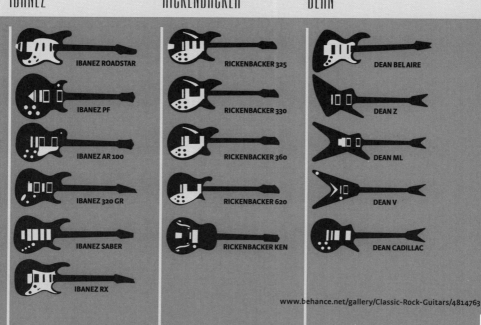

IBANEZ

- IBANEZ ROADSTAR
- IBANEZ PF
- IBANEZ AR 100
- IBANEZ 320 GR
- IBANEZ SABER
- IBANEZ RX

RICKENBACKER

- RICKENBACKER 325
- RICKENBACKER 330
- RICKENBACKER 360
- RICKENBACKER 620
- RICKENBACKER KEN

DEAN

- DEAN BEL AIRE
- DEAN Z
- DEAN ML
- DEAN V
- DEAN CADILLAC

I FOUGHT THE LAW (SORTA)

The success of ten of the best-known songs to evoke life in prison contrasted with how long their performers spent incarcerated.

2	9	8	★1	★1	★1	35	3	2	8

- Chuck Berry Thirty Days
- Bobby Fuller Four I Fought The Law
- The Rolling Stones (Jagger & Richard) We Love You
- Merle Haggard Mama Tried
- Johnny Cash Folsom Prison Blues
- Wings (Paul McCartney) Band On The Run
- The Clash Jail Guitar Doors
- Dr Dre Stranded On Death Row
- Tupac Shakur 16 On Death Row
- Akon Locked Up

'55 '65 '67 '68 '68 '74 '78 '92 '97 '04

DAYS SPENT IN PRISON

- Mann Act charges 1613
- Possession of illegal drugs 0
- Attempted robbery + jail break 3
- 1217
- Misdemeanour 1
- Possession of illegal drugs 9
- Shooting at pigeons 0.5
- Violating parole + DUI 335
- Sexual abuse 25
- Grand theft auto 1095

136

THE SOLIPSISM
INDEX

It takes a huge ego to stand up in front of thousands of strangers and entertain them, so it's to be expected that major pop stars refer to themselves in their songs. But does a truly big ego mean an equally high occurrence of self-referencing in an artist's recordings? Here are ten of the world's biggest recording stars of the past six decades graded on a solipsism index.

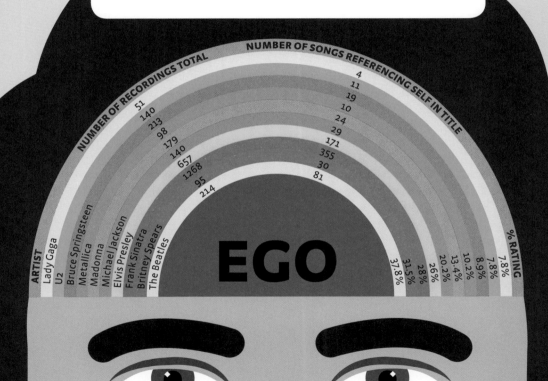

ARTIST	NUMBER OF RECORDINGS TOTAL	NUMBER OF SONGS REFERENCING SELF IN TITLE	% RATING
Lady Gaga	51	4	7.8%
U2	140	11	7.8%
Bruce Springsteen	213	19	8.9%
Metallica	98	10	10.2%
Madonna	179	24	13.4%
Michael Jackson	140	29	20.2%
Elvis Presley	657	171	26%
Frank Sinatra	1268	355	28%
Britney Spears	95	30	31.5%
The Beatles	214	81	37.8%

EGO

MADONNA IN MUSIC

MADONNA

1983

Albums sold   10,000,000

LIKE A VIRGIN

1984

⬆ 21,000,000

TRUE BLUE

1986

⬇ 17,000,000

RAY OF LIGHT

1998

Albums sold   ⬆ 16,000,000

MUSIC

2000

⬇ 15,000,000

AMERICAN LIFE

2003

⬇ 5,000,000

After scoring her first hit single worldwide in 1983, Madonna became one of the musical icons of that decade. Her career since has seen 12 studio album releases, with mixed sales results, as this graphic demonstrates.

LIKE A PRAYER

1989

↓ 15,000,000

EROTICA

1992

↓ 6,000,000

BEDTIME STORIES

1994

↓ 5,500,000

CONFESSIONS ON THE DANCE FLOOR

2005

↑ 12,000,000

HARD CANDY

2008

↓ 4,000,000

MDNA

2012

↓ 2,000,000

wikipedia.org

THE BEATLES AT SHEA STADIUM, 1965

John Lennon
1964 Rickenbacker 325 guitar
Vox Continental electric organ
2 Vox AC100 watt amplifier
head and speaker cabinets with
stands

Paul McCartney
1962 Hofner Violin bass guitar
Vox T100 watt bass amplifier
head and cabinet with stand

George Harrison
1964 Gretsch Tennessean guitar
1964 Rickenbacker 360-12 guitar
Gretsch Country Classic guitar
Vox AC100 watt amplifier head and
speaker cabinet with stand

Ringo Starr
Ludwig 55.9cm/22in bass
4-piece drum kit
Number 5 drop-T logo bass
drum head

PA
5 microphones:
two plugged into guitar amps for 'monitor'
stage sound, three into the house PA
system; one for the drums, two for vocals

The Shea Stadium 'house' PA
600-watt Altec tube amps
6 Altec 2-way A7-500 cabinets
6 EV sound columns
Altec 1567 mixer

Lighting
Stadium floodlights

THE SOUND OF LIVE MUSIC

As the legend goes, when The Beatles played at New York's Shea Stadium in 1965 for 55,000 screaming people, they had only the in-house tannoy system to spread the sound. In fact they had more than that, but as this comparison with a 21st century Paul McCartney live tour backline set-up proves, The Beatles were seriously underpowered.

PAUL MCCARTNEY TOUR, 2008

Paul McCartney
Hofner Violin bass guitar
reverse Epiphone acoustic guitar
left-handed Gibson Les Paul Sunburst electric guitar
2 VOX AC100 amplifiers
2 Mesa Boogie 400+watt amplifier heads
2 Mesa Boogie/EV Road Ready 45.7cm/18in cabinets

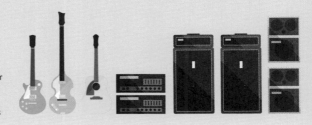

Rusty Anderson

1959 Gibson ES 335 guitar
1965 Gibson ES 335 guitar
Gibson SG electric guitar
2 Divided By 13 JRT 9/15 watt amplifiers
rack of pedal effects

Brian Ray

1959 Guild M85 bass guitar
Gretsch Double Anniversary guitar
Les Paul Sunburst electric guitar
Marshall JTM 45 amplifier head
2 2×12 closed-back Marshall cabinets

Guitar effects:

Guitarsystems pedals
Divided By 13 pedals
Demeter Compulator
Boss VB-2 Vibrato
Line 6 DL4 Delay
MM4 Modulation pedals
MXR Micro Amp
fuzz pedal

Paul 'Wix' Wickens

Native Instruments B4 organ
Titanium PowerBook
Absynth
FM7
Reaktor
Pro-52 vintage synthesizers

PA

32 MILO line array loudspeakers on 200-foot (61 metre) high cranes
7 MILO loudspeakers left, 9 right
12 UPA-1P loudspeakers front
48 700-HP subwoofers
3 left-right-center delay towers – total of 20 MICA line array loudspeakers in each
Galileo loudspeaker management system with 3 Galileo 616 units
Clair mixing console with 100 inputs
3 banks of 10 × fader controls

Lighting

59 Martin MAC 2000 spots
36 Robe ColorWash 1200E ATs
19 Coemar Infinity 1500 washes
15 MAC 2000 washes
24 Xenon 4kWs
3 Clay Paky 1.2 kW shadow spots and 6 2.5 kW Robert Juliat follow spots

Abe Laboriel Jr

Drum Workshop kit:
bass drum with accelerator
double pedal
straight snare
3 floor tom-toms
Paiste hi-hat cymbal
2 crash cymbals
2 ride cymbals

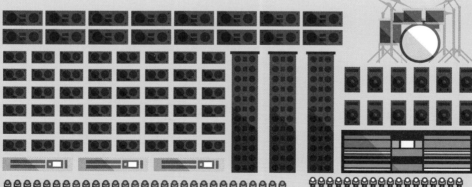

soundonsound.com, fifthbeatle.proboards.com, voxamps.com, rustyanderson.com, meyersound.com, wikipedia.org

THREE-CHORD **WONDERS**

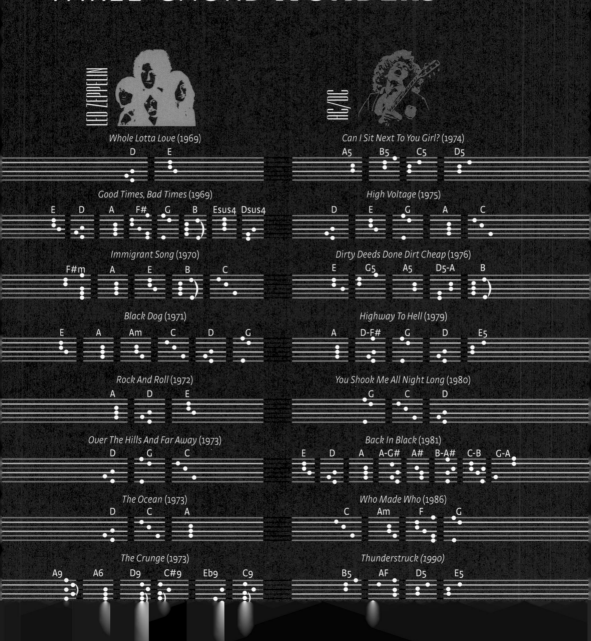

LED ZEPPELIN

Whole Lotta Love (1969)
D   E

Good Times, Bad Times (1969)
E   D   A   F#   G   B   Esus4   Dsus4

Immigrant Song (1970)
F#m   A   E   B   C

Black Dog (1971)
E   A   Am   C   D   G

Rock And Roll (1972)
A   D   E

Over The Hills And Far Away (1973)
D   G   C

The Ocean (1973)
D   C   A

The Crunge (1973)
A9   A6   D9   C#9   Eb9   C9

AC/DC

Can I Sit Next To You Girl? (1974)
A5   B5   C5   D5

High Voltage (1975)
D   E   G   A   C

Dirty Deeds Done Dirt Cheap (1976)
E   G5   A5   D5-A   B

Highway To Hell (1979)
A   D-F#   G   D   E5

You Shook Me All Night Long (1980)
G   C   D

Back In Black (1981)
E   D   A   A-G#   A#   B-A#   C-B   G-A

Who Made Who (1986)
C   Am   F   G

Thunderstruck (1990)
B5   AF   D5   E5

It's long been a staple of rock music that a guitar band needs to know only three chords in order to make good, loud, raucous rock'n'roll. Examining the chords used throughout the careers of four of the best, Led Zeppelin, AC/DC, The Ramones and The Scorpions, that doesn't seem to be true.

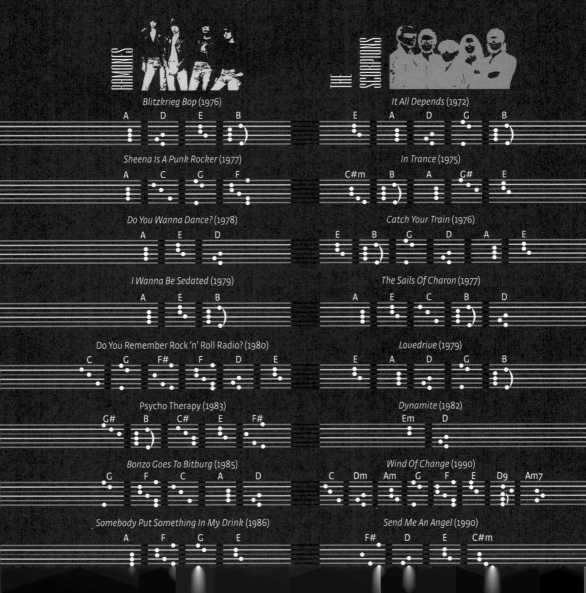

Blitzkrieg Bop (1976)
A D E B

It All Depends (1972)
E A D G B

Sheena Is A Punk Rocker (1977)
A C G F

In Trance (1975)
C#m B A G# E

Do You Wanna Dance? (1978)
A E D

Catch Your Train (1976)
E B G D A E

I Wanna Be Sedated (1979)
A E B

The Sails Of Charon (1977)
A E C B D

Do You Remember Rock 'n' Roll Radio? (1980)
C G F# F D E

Lovedrive (1979)
E A D G B

Psycho Therapy (1983)
G# B C# E F#

Dynamite (1982)
Em D

Bonzo Goes To Bitburg (1985)
G F C A D

Wind Of Change (1990)
C Dm Am G F E D9 Am7

Somebody Put Something In My Drink (1986)
A F G E

Send Me An Angel (1990)
F# D E C#m

IS IT OVER WHEN THE
FAT LADY SINGS?

In opera the 'fat lady' is usually the female lead who'll die, but before she goes will get to sing an aria (alone). However, in the majority of these 30 of the most often performed works (according to operabase.com), that isn't the case.

Composer | Title | *Character*

TOTAL SINGS LAST
AND DIES = 7

Verdi | La Traviata | *Violeta*

Puccini | Tosca | *Floria Tosca*

Puccini | Madame Butterfly | *Cio-Cio San*

Verdi | Rigoletto | *Gilda*

Verdi | Nabucco | *Abigaille*

Verdi | Il Trovatore | *Leonara*

Wagner | Der Fliegende Holländer | *Senta*

TOTAL SINGS LAST
AND LIVES = 3

Mozart | The Marriage Of Figaro | *Countess Rosina*

Puccini | Turandot | *Princess Turandot*

Rossini | La Cenerentola | *Cenerentola*

operbase.com, wikipedia.org

TOTAL DOESN'T SING LAST **AND DIES = 8**

Bizet | Carmen | *Carmen*

Puccini | La Bohème | *Mimi*

Verdi | Aida | *Aida*

Humperdinck | Hansel Und Gretel | *The witch*

Leoncavallo | Pagliacci | *Nadda*

Donizetti | Lucia di Lammermoor | *Lucia*

Verdi | Otello | *Desdemona*

Verdi | Macbeth | *Lady Macbeth*

TOTAL DOESN'T SING LAST **AND LIVES = 12**

Mozart | The Magic Flute | *Pamina*

Rossini | The Barber Of Seville | *Rosina*

Mozart | Don Giovanni | *Elvira*

Johan Strauss II | Die Fledermaus | *Rosalinde*

Donizetti | L'Elisir d'Amore | *Adina*

Mozart | Cosi Fan Tutti | *Fiordiligi / Dorabella*

Tchaikovsky | Eugene Onegin | *Tatyana*

Lehar | Die Lustige Witwe | *Hanna Glawari*

Mascagni | Cavalleria Rusticana | *Santuzza*

Verdi | Un Ballo In Maschera | *Amelia*

Mozart | Die Entführung | *Konstanze*

Wagner | Die Walküre | *Brünnhilde*

DIVAS come in all sizes:
Dress sizes (US/UK) of renowned sopranos

1/4 Maria Callas

2/6 Marina Rebeka
Danielle de Niese
Kiri Te Kanawa

4/8 Anna Netrobko
Katherine Jenkins
Elina Garanča

6/10 Renée Fleming

8/12 Celine Byrne

10/14 Deborah Voigt

HIP-HOP BY NUMBERS

Since its evolution from street parties in the Bronx circa 1973, hip-hop music has grown to become one of the dominant forces in music around the world. Its roots remain in America, however, as the figures for the top ten best-selling albums of all time demonstrate. The numbers also suggest that the music has lost some overall popularity since the early 2000s.

THE AUDIENCE

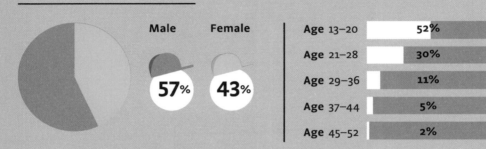

Male 57%   **Female** 43%

Age 13–20	52%
Age 21–28	30%
Age 29–36	11%
Age 37–44	5%
Age 45–52	2%

TOP TEN BEST-SELLING ALBUMS OF ALL TIME

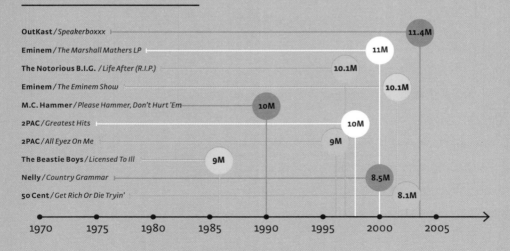

OutKast / *Speakerboxxx* — 11.4M
Eminem / *The Marshall Mathers LP* — 11M
The Notorious B.I.G. / *Life After (R.I.P.)* — 10.1M
Eminem / *The Eminem Show* — 10.1M
M.C. Hammer / *Please Hammer, Don't Hurt 'Em* — 10M
2PAC / *Greatest Hits* — 10M
2PAC / *All Eyez On Me* — 9M
The Beastie Boys / *Licensed To Ill* — 9M
Nelly / *Country Grammar* — 8.5M
50 Cent / *Get Rich Or Die Tryin'* — 8.1M

1970 1975 1980 1985 1990 1995 2000 2005

www.hiphop365.com, www.wikipedia.org, www.audionetwork.com, www.celebritynetworth.com, www.beforeitsnews.com

RICHEST HIP-HOP STARS

P. Diddy

$590M

Jay-Z

$540M

Dr Dre

$360M

50 Cent

$260M

Birdman

$170M

Snoop Dogg

$150M

Eminem

$140M

Lil Wayne

$115M

Kanye West

$120M

Nicki Minaj

$100M

THE NEW ECONOMICS
OF THE MUSIC INDUSTRY

*As technology advances every day, new markets have been created
for listening to music. These new markets have transitioned music
from ownership to access and affect not only user behaviour towards
the music industry, but the entire economics of the industry.*

POWER OF ARTIST

is changing due to
new music platforms

**Individual artists can make tens of thousands of dollars a
month on YouTube.**

**Individual artists can make more money on an individual
basis from YouTube than they do from iTunes.**

Examples of bands
that left their
labels and made
their own label

OK GO	TRAIL OF DEAD
KID CUDI	ALKALINE TRIO
CAKE	OASIS
PRINCE	WHITE STRIPES
WILCO	NINE INCH NAILS
GRETCHEN WILSON	RADIOHEAD
THE ROLLING STONES	

www.pastemagazine.com

Today, an artist can pay a service like TuneCore to be included in the
iTunes store. At that point, after Apple takes its cut, the entire 90 cents
goes to the artist.

TuneCore charges $50 a year, and takes no slice of the sale. An artist needs
about 5,000 plays for a song on Spotify or about 56 downloads of a song on
iTunes to break even.

www.thenextweb.com

As the music industry enters into a new era for listening to music, artists,
labels and retailers need to adapt their dynamic to continue making
money. They must now account for the multitude of platforms that
the music can be heard from.

www.priscilamendoza.mx/118810/1175471/design-management/the-new-economics-of-the-music-industry,
www.rollingstone.com, www.pastemagazine.com, www.thenextweb.com

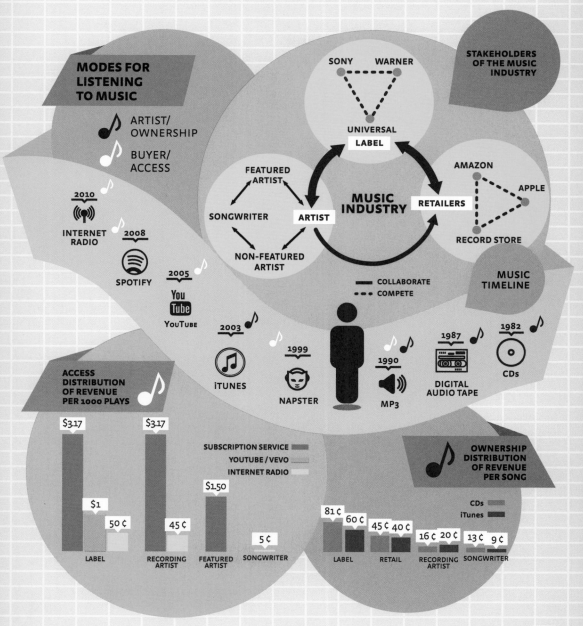

MODES FOR LISTENING TO MUSIC

🎵 ARTIST/OWNERSHIP
🎵 BUYER/ACCESS

2010 INTERNET RADIO
2008 SPOTIFY
2005 YouTube
2003 iTUNES
1999 NAPSTER
1990 MP3
1987 DIGITAL AUDIO TAPE
1982 CDs

STAKEHOLDERS OF THE MUSIC INDUSTRY

SONY   WARNER
UNIVERSAL
LABEL

MUSIC INDUSTRY

FEATURED ARTIST
SONGWRITER
ARTIST
NON-FEATURED ARTIST

RETAILERS

AMAZON
APPLE
RECORD STORE

—— COLLABORATE
---- COMPETE

MUSIC TIMELINE

ACCESS DISTRIBUTION OF REVENUE PER 1000 PLAYS

SUBSCRIPTION SERVICE
YOUTUBE / VEVO
INTERNET RADIO

$3.17 / $1 / 50¢ — LABEL
$3.17 / 45¢ — RECORDING ARTIST
$1.50 — FEATURED ARTIST
5¢ — SONGWRITER

OWNERSHIP DISTRIBUTION OF REVENUE PER SONG

CDs
iTunes

81¢ / 60¢ — LABEL
45¢ / 40¢ — RETAIL
16¢ / 20¢ — RECORDING ARTIST
13¢ / 9¢ — SONGWRITER

ORIGINAL SOUNDTRACK

While sales of original soundtrack albums in the 1950s and 1960s were decent, the really successful ones were either for stage shows that became movies, or single-artist vehicles such as Elvis Presley's Blue Hawaii *or The Beatles'* A Hard Day's Night *and* Help!. *At the end of the 1970s, though, OSTs became enormously successful as compilation albums when* Saturday Night Fever *became one of the biggest-selling albums of all time.*

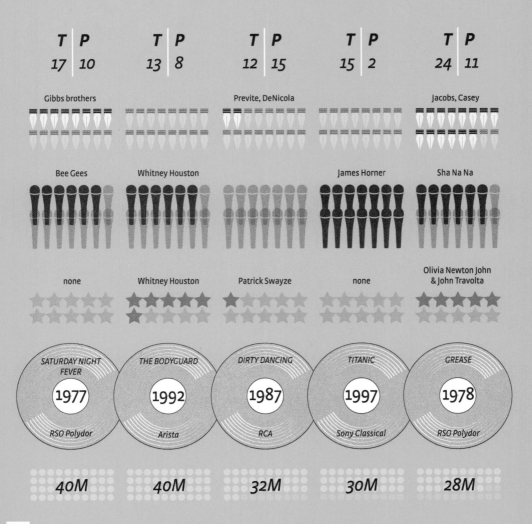

T	P		T	P		T	P		T	P		T	P
17	10		13	8		12	15		15	2		24	11

Gibbs brothers

Previte, DeNicola

Jacobs, Casey

Bee Gees

Whitney Houston

James Horner

Sha Na Na

Whitney Houston

Patrick Swayze

Olivia Newton John & John Travolta

SATURDAY NIGHT FEVER — 1977 — RSO Polydor

THE BODYGUARD — 1992 — Arista

DIRTY DANCING — 1987 — RCA

TITANIC — 1997 — Sony Classical

GREASE — 1978 — RSO Polydor

40M   40M   32M   30M   28M

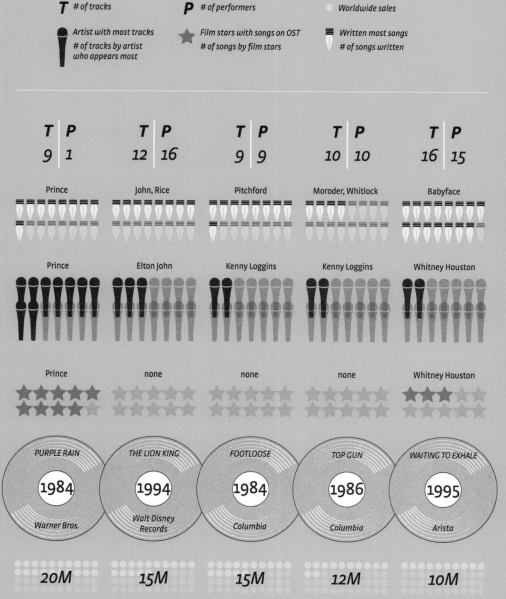

T # of tracks **P** # of performers ● Worldwide sales

🎤 Artist with most tracks / # of tracks by artist who appears most

★ Film stars with songs on OST / # of songs by film stars

≣ Written most songs / # of songs written

T	P		T	P		T	P		T	P		T	P
9	1		12	16		9	9		10	10		16	15

Prince · John, Rice · Pitchford · Moroder, Whitlock · Babyface

Prince · Elton John · Kenny Loggins · Kenny Loggins · Whitney Houston

Prince · none · none · none · Whitney Houston

PURPLE RAIN **1984** Warner Bros.

THE LION KING **1994** Walt Disney Records

FOOTLOOSE **1984** Columbia

TOP GUN **1986** Columbia

WAITING TO EXHALE **1995** Arista

20M · 15M · 15M · 12M · 10M

wikipedia.org

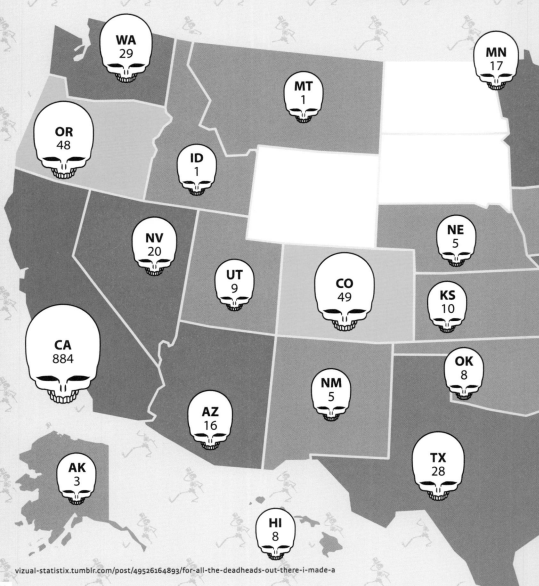

FOLLOWING
THE DEAD

WA
29

MN
17

MT
1

OR
48

ID
1

NE
5

NV
20

UT
9

CO
49

KS
10

CA
884

NM
5

OK
8

AZ
16

AK
3

TX
28

HI
8

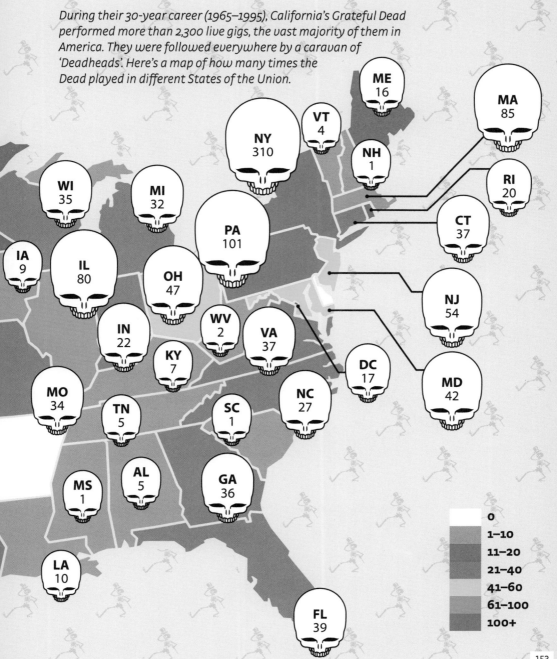

During their 30-year career (1965–1995), California's Grateful Dead performed more than 2,300 live gigs, the vast majority of them in America. They were followed everywhere by a caravan of 'Deadheads'. Here's a map of how many times the Dead played in different States of the Union.

ME 16
VT 4
MA 85
NY 310
NH 1
RI 20
CT 37
WI 35
MI 32
PA 101
NJ 54
IA 9
IL 80
OH 47
WV 2
VA 37
DC 17
MD 42
IN 22
KY 7
NC 27
MO 34
TN 5
SC 1
GA 36
MS 1
AL 5
LA 10
FL 39

0
1–10
11–20
21–40
41–60
61–100
100+

153

100 YEARS OF **ROCK**

The roots of contemporary popular music are to be found in a number of cities around the world. Here's where different sub-genres emerged from, plus the key contribution each made.

EUROPE

1957
London,
Skiffle/
Lonnie
Donegan

1961
Liverpool,
Merseybeat/
The Beatles

1965
London,
Mod/
The Who

1966
Canterbury,
Progressive
Rock/Soft
Machine

1968
Wolverhampton,
Heavy Metal/
Black Sabbath

1970
Düsseldorf,
Krautrock/
Kraftwerk

1970
London,
Glam Rock/
David
Bowie

1972
Munich,
Synth-pop/
Giorgio
Moroder

1975
Cleveland,
Adult
Oriented
Rock Radio/
Fleetwood
Mac

1976
West Berlin,
New Age
Music/
Tangerine
Dream

1976
London,
Punk Rock/
The Sex
Pistols

1976
London,
New
Wave/Elvis
Costello

1977
Paris,
World
Music/
Womad

1982

1982
Manchester,
Indie/The
Smiths

1987
Bristol,
Trip-Hop/
Massive
Attack

1991
Amsterdam,
Eurodance/
2 Unlimited

1992
London,
Drum'N'
Bass/Goldie

2001
London,
Grime/Dizzee
Rascal

REST

1964 **Kingston, Jamaica,** Studio One/
Bob Marley And The Wailers

1972 **Tokyo,** Electro Rock/Tomita

1992 **Seoul City,** K-Pop Seo Taiji

1959
**Muscle
Shoals,**
Fame
Studio,
R&B/Arthur
Alexander

1960
New York,
Soul/Sam
Cooke

1961
Memphis,
Stax Records,
Soul/Booker
T & The M.G.s

USA

1914	**St Louis,** Blues/W.C. Handy
1925	**Nashville,** Country Music/ WSM Barn Dance (Grand Ole Opry)
1927	**Chicago,** Folk Blues/Big Bill Broonzy
1927	**Asheville, N. Carolina,** Country Music/ Jimmie Rodgers
1932	**Clarksdale, Mississippi,** Blues/ Robert Johnson
1938	**Kansas City,** Be-bop Jazz/Charlie Parker
1939	**Tulsa, Oklahoma,** Western Swing/ Bob Wills
1943	**Cincinatti,** R&B/King Records/Moon Mullican; Federal Records/James Brown
1945	**New Orleans,** R&B/ J&M Studios/Fats Domino
1947	**Los Angeles,** R&B/Imperial Records/Huey 'Piano' Smith; Specialty Records/Little Richard
1947	**New York,** R&B/Atlantic Records/ Big Joe Turner
1947	**New Orleans,** R&B/Roy Brown/ Good Rocking Tonight
1948	**Los Angeles,** R&B/Louis Jordan
1948	**Shreveport, Louisiana,** Country/ Louisiana Hayride/Hank Williams
1949	**Houston,** R&B/Peacock Records/ Big Mama Thornton
1949	**San Francisco,** Beat Poetry KPFA Radio Station/Allen Ginsberg's Howl
1952	**Philadelphia,** Rock 'n' Roll/ American Bandstand, TV show
1952	**Memphis,** Sun Records, Rock 'n' Roll/ Elvis Presley
1952	**Chicago,** Urban Blues/Muddy Waters, John Lee Hooker
1952	**Cleveland, Ohio,** Rock 'n' Roll Radio/ Alan Freed
1953	**Memphis,** Rockabilly/Carl Perkins
1956	**Clovis, New Mexico,** Rock 'n' Roll/ Norman Petty Studio, Buddy Holly
1957	**New York,** Pop/Brill Building, Leiber And Stoller
1959	**Detroit,** Soul/Motown Records, Smokey Robinson & The Miracles

Diagonal branches:

1961	Los Angeles, Surf Pop/ The Beach Boys/Surfin'
1961	New York, Folk Rock/Bob Dylan
1963	Los Angeles, Pop/Gold Star Studios, Phil Spector Wall Of Sound
1964	Portland, Oregon, Garage Rock/ The Kingsmen
1965	Cincinatti, Funk/James Brown
1965	New Orleans, Funk/Allen Toussaint/ The Meters
1965	Washington D.C., Go-Go/Chuck Brown & The Soul Searchers
1968	San Francisco, Psychedelic Rock/ Jefferson Airplane
1968	San Francisco, Hard Rock/ Iron Butterfly
1971	Austin, Texas, Blues Rock/ Johnny Winter
1973	Philadelphia, Philly Soul/International Records

Lower diagonal branches:

1973	Miami, Disco/TK Records, KC & The Sunshine Band
1973	New York Bronx, Hip-hop/ DJ Kool Herc
1975	New York, Punk Rock/The Ramones
1979	Minneapolis, Pop, Paisley Park/Prince
1983	Athens, Georgia, Alt Rock/REM
1983	Detroit, Techno/Derrick May
1984	Chicago, House Music/Frankie Knuckles
1986	Minneapolis, New Jack Swing/Janet Jackson
1986	Los Angeles, Gangsta Rap/Ice-T
1987	Chicago, Acid House/Phuture
1987	Seattle, Grunge/Nirvana

JESUSLAND ON YOUTUBE

In a search for videos of songs featuring the name Jesus on YouTube on Easter Sunday, the different musical genres worked out as shown. Alt-rockers love Him more than twice as much as country singers, it appears.

ALT-ROCK

NUMBER OF VIDEOS ON YOUTUBE

40

30

20

10

COUNTRY

ROCK

POP

BLUES

RAP

HEAVY METAL

FOLK

DANCE

COMEDY

SOUL

MUSIC GENRE

Actual income

Live Nation deal

THE 360 DEGREES OF **JAY-Z**

This breakdown of the deal brokered between Live Nation and Jay-Z shows why it works for both parties.

$14m sales of 'The Blueprint' album
$18m sales of 'Watch The Throne' album
$2m support slot with U2 tour
$2m 'Home To Home' tour
$34.2m 2008 tour with Mary J. Blige
$48m 2009 tour

$20m advance against publishing, licensing and producing fees
$25m 'signing on' fee
$25m advance against tour, merch and related income
$10m advance for first album of a 3-album deal
$10m advance for second album of a 3-album deal
$10m advance for third album of a 3-album deal

wikipedia.org, Billboard, New York Times

WHERE **CLASSICAL MUSIC** COMES FROM

What we now know as 'classical music' began in the 17th century in central Europe, and developed from city to city as individual composers came to the fore. Here are the major composers of each period of classical music and the cities where they were born.

Terry Riley
Colfax, CA 1935–
USA

LaMonte Young
Bern, Idaho 1935–
USA

John Adams
Worcester, MA 1947–
USA

Amy Beach
Henniker, NH 1867–1944
USA

Aaron Copland
New York, NY 1900–1990
USA

Charles Ives
Danbury, CT
1875–1954 USA

Morton Feldman
New York, NY 1926–1987
USA

Terence Blanchard
New Orleans, LA 1962–
USA

George Gershwin
New York, NY 1898–1937
USA

Steve Reich
New York, NY 1936–
USA

John Cage
Los Angeles, CA 1912–1992
USA

John Philip Sousa
Washington, DC 1854–1932
USA

Bernard Herrmann
New York, NY 1911–1975
USA

Miguel Bernal Jimenez
Morelia, Michoacán 1910–1956
Mexico

 BAROQUE
(1600–1760)

 CLASSICAL
(1730–1820)

 ROMANTIC
(1815–1910)

 MODERN
(1890–1930)

 20TH CENTURY
(1901–2000)

 CONTEMPORARY
(1975–present)

Heitor Villa-lobos
Rio de Janeiro 1887–1959
Brazil

Violeta Parra
San Carlos 1917–1967
Chile

Alberto Ginastera
Buenos Aires 1916–1983
Argentina

Juan Carlos Pax
Buenos Aires 1901–1972
Argentina

Astor Piazzolla
Mar del Plata 1921–1992
Argentina

Juan Pedro Esnaola
Buenos Aires 1808–1880
Argentina

Jean Sibelius
Hameenlinna 1865–1957
Finland

Benjamin Britten
Lowestoft 1913–1976
England

Carl Nielsen
Odense 1865–1931
Denmark

Sergei Rachmaninoff
Veliky Nougorod 1883–1943
Russia

John Tavener
London 1947–2012
England

Johann Sebastian Bach
Leipzig 1685–1750
Germany

Carl Philipp Emanuel Bach
Weimar 1714–1788
Germany

Gustav Holst
Cheltenham 1770–1827
England

Dmitri Shostakovich
Saint Petersburg 1906–1975
Russia

George Frideric Handel
Halle 1685–1759
Germany

Arvo Part
Paide 1935–
Estonia

Ludwig Van Beethoven
Bonn 1770–1827
Germany

Frederic Chopin
Zelazowa Wola 1810–1849
Poland

Claude Debussy
Saint Hermain En Laye
1862–1918 France

Karl-Heinz Stockhausen
Modrath 1928–2007
Germany

Henryk Gorecki
Czernica 1933–2010
Poland

Wolfgang Amadeus Mozart
Vienna 1756–1791
Austria

Béla Bartók
Sannicolau Mare 1881–1945
Romania

Maurice Ravel
Ciboure 1875–1937
France

Arnold Schoenberg
Vienna 1874–1951
Austria

Franz Schubert
Vienna 1797–1828
Austria

Sergei Prokofiev
Sontsouka 1891–1953
Ukraine

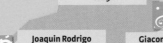

Gaezano Donizetti
Bergamo 1797–1848
Italy

Antonio Vivaldi
Venice 1678–1741
Italy

Joaquin Rodrigo
Sagunto 1901–1999
Spain

Giacomo Puccini
Lucca 1858–1924
Italy

Nie Er
Kunming 1912–1935
China

Credits

Produced by Essential Works Ltd
essentialworks.co.uk

Essential Works

Art Director: Gemma Wilson
Supervising Editor:
Mal Peachey
Editor: Julia Halford
Researchers: Russell Beecher,
Daniel Collum, George Edgeller,
Maudie Phillimore
Layout: Ben Cracknell

Octopus Books

Editorial Director:
Trevor Davies

Production Controller:
Sarah Connelly

Designers/Illustrators

Marc Morera Agustí (20–21, 58–59)
Federica Bonfanti (10–11, 32–33, 158–159)
Kuo Kang Chen (14–17)
Ian Cowles (34–35, 74–75)
Giulia De Amicis (66–67)
Barbara Doherty (12–13, 26–27, 62–63, 88–89, 96–97, 102–103, 114–115, 124–125, 126, 138–139, 142–143, 156)
Wayne Dorrington (92–93, 122–123)
Christian Enache (86–87)
Wojciech Grabalowski (56–57, 76–77, 150–151, 154–155)
Nick Graves (36–37, 48–49, 60–61, 70–71)
Lorena Guerra (18–19, 30–31, 46–47, 82–83, 108–109, 110–111)
Jamie Gurnell (100)
Natasha Hellegouarch (54–55, 104–105)
Erwin Hilao (80–81)
David Hurtado (118–119)

Seth Kadish (42–43)
Yann Le Neve (40–41)
Stephen Lillie (72–73, 112–113, 130–131)
Mish Maudsley (84–85)
Priscila Mendoza, Yazmin Alanis (144–145)
Priscila Mendoza, Michael Denman, Bhavika Shah (148–149)
Kaira Mezulis (90–91)
Milkwhale.com (152–153)
Ahmed Naseer aka Med Nes (64–65)
Aleksandar Savic (52, 53, 94–95, 127, 140–141, 146–147)
Yael Shinkar (50–51, 68–69, 106–107)
Matt Veal (120–121)
Fedor Velyaminov (22–23)
Sergio Villarreal (134–135)
Ryan Welch (44–45)
Gemma Wilson (38–39, 78–79, 116–117, 128–129, 132–133, 137)
Anil Yanik (98–99, 136)